THROUGH A CHILD'S EYES

How Classroom Design Inspires Learning and Wonder

Sandra Duncan, EdD, Jody Martin,
and Sally Haughey

Gryphon House
Lewisville, NC

Library of Congress Cataloging-in-Publication Data

Names: Duncan, Sandra, 1945- author.
Title: Through a child's eyes : how classroom design inspires learning and
   wonder / Sandra Duncan, Jody Martin, and Sally Haughey.
Description: Lewisville, N.C. : Gryphon House, Inc., [2018] | Includes
   bibliographical references and index.
Identifiers: LCCN 2018024649 | ISBN 9780876597965 (pbk.)
Subjects: LCSH: Classrooms--Planning. | Classroom environment.
Classification: LCC LB3325.C5 D86 2018 | DDC 371.6/21--dc23 LC record available at https://lccn.loc.gov/2018024649

Bulk Purchase

Gryphon House books are available for special premiums and sales promotions as well as for fund-raising use. Special editions or book excerpts also can be created to specifications. For details, call 800.638.0928.

Disclaimer

Gryphon House, Inc., cannot be held responsible for damage, mishap, or injury incurred during the use of or because of activities in this book. Appropriate and reasonable caution and adult supervision of children involved in activities and corresponding to the age and capability of each child involved are recommended at all times. Do not leave children unattended at any time. Observe safety and caution at all times.

Acknowledgements

We are deeply grateful to the many people who shared their knowledge, insight, and inspiration for this book including children and teachers, centers and schools, and early childhood advocates, experts, and colleagues. Their innovative ideas are inspiring and motivating. We also want to express gratitude to our friends and family for their support and encouragement as we worked diligently to bring this book to life. To all of you, our profound appreciation, gratitude, and thanks:

Anchorage Park, Barbara Shore, Bianca Woodberry, Blaine and Hannah Wheaton, Brandi Dietz, Child Development and Learning Laboratory of Central Michigan University, Cheryl Dickson, Children's Home + Aid, Debbie Applebaum, Downtown Baltimore Child Care, Education Station, Gillian McAuliffe, Hagy Center for Young Children, Heather Parker Goetzinger, Homewood Early Learning, Irvine Nature Preschool, Isaiah Huppenthal, iSmile Alam Atelier School, Jen Sticken, Jenni Caldwell, John Martin, John Wyrick, Julie Ranalli, Just for Tots #2, Kay Koern, Kenzie Clendennen, Kim Winegart, Liberty O'Connor, Linda Wywiałkowski, Lycel Arboleda, Patty Eaton, Margo Sipes, Mary Clare Munger, Melanie Vega, Messiah Moravian Preschool, Milgard Child Development Center at Pierce College, Monique Heeg, Nancy Manewith, Nature's Way Preschool, Nicole Hill, Padyrna Patet, Pampa Community Day Care Center, Region 16 Head Start, Ronnie's Preschool, Rosa Parks Early Childhood Center, Sharyl Robin, Sierra Elizabeth Austin, Sue Pennix, Summit School, Susan Jones, The Adventure Club, The Board of Jewish Education Early Childhood Center at B'nai Tikvah, The Little School, Veronica Green, Vicki Wright, Victor Quinoes, Waverly Schreiber, Roong Aroon School. , Kids Country, Melissa Henningin, Chris Burkeholder, Mickey McGilvery, Hope's Home, Gary Bilezikian, Heidi Bilezikian, Guidecraft, Community Playthings, Rhonda Johnson, Elyssa Nelson, Child Educational Center, The Little School, Jennifer Dock, Children's Home and Aid, Harpreet Kaur, Sierra Elizabeth Austin, and Janel Boese.

Foreword

The power of space.

It's an expression that brings to mind images of the Grand Canyon, Niagara Falls, and of the sun setting over a magnificent mountain range—settings that invoke feelings of awe and humility.

But what of the everyday spaces, the classrooms, offices, and kitchens where the bulk of our lives are spent? Do these spaces not also affect us in profound and far-reaching ways? Think back to a classroom where you attended elementary school or perhaps your grandmother's basement or the vacant lot where you learned to ride a bike. What would such memories be without the surrounding environments? And would your memories be nearly as powerful without the sights, sounds, and smells of those places? What these memories all have in common is that we experienced them as children. It is classrooms, playgrounds, and lunchrooms that helped shape our experiences and selves—some for good, others perhaps not as much. Could there be a few basic principles at work in the places we remember most fondly? Can we intentionally design space in such a way as to enhance our learning and memories? The answer is yes. We can design spaces that inspire learning and a child's sense of wonder. The key is to preserve the magic and wonder of childhood by creating places that allow children to simply be children. It is what young children need and what they deserve.

—Sandra Duncan, Jody Martin, and Sally Haughey

Table of Contents

1

The Power of Space: Understanding the Importance of Classroom Design

The catalyst that converts any physical location—any environment if you will—into a place, is the process of experiencing deeply. A place is a piece of the whole environment that has been claimed by feelings . . . We are homesick for places.

—Alan Gussow, *A Sense of Place*

Special spaces often become so because of personal memories, such as your childhood home or the spot where you fell in love. Some spaces, however, are special because they were created for specific uses and purposes. A library is a space to hold books along with other resources, and its purpose is to encourage literacy and offer information. A natural history museum is intended to educate visitors about the world. Clearly, the specificities and intentions of any designed space impact our emotions and behavior. Such places can awe young and old alike. Consider, for example, the Sistine Chapel.

The Sistine Chapel is a redesign of an older existing chapel in Vatican City. Completed between 1477 and 1481, the Sistine Chapel is renowned for its frescoes painted by a team of artists including Michelangelo Buonarotti, who painted the famous ceiling fresco. The design intention of the Sistine Chapel is to inspire worship. It is a sanctuary for people to find deep spiritual comfort and inspiration. The chapel's art and architecture bathe worshippers in serenity, beauty, and peace.

Just as the Sistine Chapel is intentionally designed to serve a purpose, so must early childhood classrooms be intentional. Classrooms are meant to inspire children to grow and become their very best, and intentional classroom design is vital for promoting this inspiration. Children deserve thoughtfully and intentionally designed classrooms. What are our purposes for teaching young children? What would the environment look like in fulfilling those purposes? What essential understandings lay the foundation for designing spaces for young children?

Essential Understandings of Classroom Design

As educators and designers of early childhood environments, we must examine our ideas about how children reach their maximum potential. Then we can decide which types of environments most effectively support children's growth. There are critical components—essential understandings—of classroom design that help to foster children's capacity to reach their maximum potential.

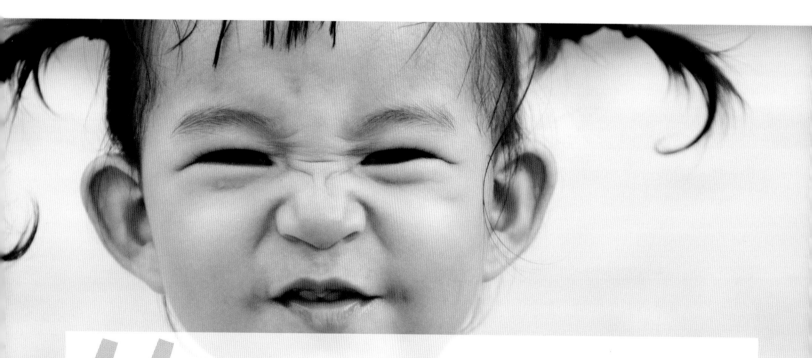

“Children are miracles. Believing that every child is a miracle can transform the way we design for children's care. When we invite a miracle into our lives we prepare ourselves and the environment around us . . . We make it our job to create, with reverence and gratitude, a space that is worthy of a miracle!

—Anita Rui Olds, author and designer

"Children are the spark plug in the engine of life, the motivation behind our best deeds, and the evidence for hope in the future.

—Ina Hughs, Foreword, *From My Side: Being a Child*

Essential Understanding 1: Honor Children First and Foremost

Honor is an important word. It is about respect, empathy, acceptance, and patience. Classrooms designed to honor children are environments filled with choices, meaningful experiences, respectful interactions and communications, and relevant collaborations. Children are treated as important, competent contributors. Each child's voice is heard, and all opinions are valued. Children's work is respected and displayed with pride, integrity, and thoughtfulness. In classrooms of honor, the language and culture of each child is revered. Children's lives and identities are supported with dignity. Families are welcomed. Most importantly, honoring children means giving them a chance to be whoever they want, whatever they dream, wherever their journey takes them.

Essential Understanding 2: Cherish Children's Spaces

Early childhood practitioners nurture and support young children, but they often fail to consider how to extend this nurturing impulse to the classroom. The impulse to nurture the child comes more naturally than the impulse to nurture the space. If we truly believe in honoring children through the environment, then we must cherish the classroom space. This means creating environments that preserve children's child-like qualities—laughter, joy, inquisitiveness, curiosity, playfulness, innocence, and delight—not only in the world around them, but in their very selves. In these spaces, young children can sing, dance, build, paint, and share stories.

> We place enormous value on the role of the environment as a motivating and animating force . . . that produces a sense of well-being and security.
>
> —Loris Malaguzzi, founder of the Reggio Emilia philosophy and pedagogy

Essential Understanding 3: Celebrate the Spirit of Place

All children have a deep need for special places. Do you remember a favorite childhood place? These places hold a sense of wonder for us. As young children, these places enchanted us—whether our special space was a hand-built fort made of odd pieces of wood found in the garage, a secret meeting place under a big bush in the backyard, or the housekeeping center in the preschool classroom. We wanted to return to these special places time and again.

> A spirited place enlivens the soul.
>
> —Anita Rui Olds, *Child Care Design Guide*

We vividly remember tiny details about our special places—the sights, smells, and textures. The Latin term *genius loci* means "the spirit of a place." Anita Rui Olds asserts in her book *Child Care Design Guide*, "Our goal as designers is to create places of freedom and delight where the enchantments and mysteries of childhood can be given full expression. A spirited place satisfies children's souls."

What is the essence of a spirited classroom for young children? It respects and encourages children's inherent drive to discover the world around them. Such a space is filled with interesting objects designed for sensory exploration that beckon children to investigate, manipulate, and collaborate with others.

Essential Understanding 4: Create Islands of Balance and Beauty

Have you ever spent the day near water—a pond, stream, lake, or ocean? The feel of the breeze, the sound of water lapping on shore, and the earthy scent wafting through the air? There is an inherent beauty and balance of nature that touches us deeply. Beauty has the power to give us a sense of peace and pleasure, and it is an essential force in our lives. This desire for beauty is not exclusive to adults. Author and educator Ruth Wilson believes that young children also need and seek beauty.

It really goes beyond the notion that children need beauty. Children *deserve* beauty. They deserve more than the mere walls, door, ceiling, and floor of the classroom. Children deserve more than institutional rooms with hard surfaces and cookie-cutter room arrangements, more than plastic and commercially purchased toys and equipment. Early childhood classrooms should have natural light, fresh air, growing plants, and fresh flowers. Children deserve beautiful nuggets of nature to explore and investigate. Classrooms of physical beauty foster aesthetic sensitivity and give children a deeper connection to the wonder of life.

> When we experience the beautiful, there is a sense of homecoming.
>
> —John O'Donohue, *Beauty*

The Power of Intentional Classroom Environments

The classroom is powerful. Its space has the capacity to regulate children's behaviors either positively or negatively. The classroom environment also has the power to nurture (or stifle) young children's growth and development. The environment significantly influences the quality of social interactions among children and adults. This effect is so significant that it has been deemed the "third teacher" by Reggio Emilia educator Lella Gandini. The types of materials available in the classroom, including the furniture, and the way in which they are arranged influence how children act, react, learn, and grow. Prakash Nair, Randall Fielding, and Jeffery Lackney believe that the power to affect children's development is rooted in more than arrangement and classroom materials. In their book *The Language of School Design: Design Patterns for 21st Century Schools*, they explain how the ideas of designers, educators, and architects can converge. The authors suggest designing schools with learning suites and studios where small groups of children can gather to collaborate and create. The authors suggest making classrooms flexible so spaces can be quickly reconfigured to support the emerging interests of the learners. They suggest breaking down the walls to let the sunshine in.

Our surroundings have a powerful influence on how we feel, act, and respond to the world. The growing field of neuro-architecture has confirmed that a thoughtfully planned environment is critical to a person's well-being. By researching how the body and brain respond to different features such as layout, furnishings, lighting, and color, science has proven that our overall health and well-being is directly affected by the arrangement of our personal spaces. Sarah Williams Goldhagen, professor at Harvard University's Graduate School of Design, has conducted research on how our brains register our surrounding environments. In her book *Welcome to Your World: How Built Environments Shape Our Lives*, Goldhagen calls this idea *embodied cognition*. She believes that our surroundings shape our lives and nudge us to think, behave, and feel in certain ways. Other researchers, such as Rikard Kuller, Seifeddin Bailai, Thorbjorn Laike, and Bryan Mikelldes, have studied embodied cognition with their research on the effects of light and color on the psychological moods of adults. They found a clear connection between participants' moods and their perceptions about the levels of light they were experiencing. Participants' moods were at the lowest when they perceived the lighting was too dark and, conversely, at the highest when they perceived the lighting as just right. Positive moods dropped off, however, when participants perceived the lighting as too bright.

Likewise, Salford University emeritus professor Peter Barrett and his colleagues have studied the connection between space and children's well-being through the potential of positive spaces. Many young children are not yet adept at expressing their feelings or self-regulating their bodies. Therefore, it is the early childhood practitioner's responsibility to create classroom spaces that positively influence children.

Environmental Practices

According to the Division for Early Childhood of the Council for Exceptional Children, the concept of environmental practices refers to all factors of a space, including equipment, materials, routines, and activities that teachers can intentionally infuse, create, change, or alter to support children's learning. As far back as 1969, Sybil Kritchevsky, Elizabeth Prescott, and Lee Walling analyzed child care settings and determined that classroom design influences the behaviors and social interactions of both children and teachers. The researchers observed the physical space's arrangement and how children navigated through the classroom, worked with the materials, and interacted with others. Kritchevsky, Prescott, and Walling's research illustrated how a thoughtfully designed classroom positively affected children's actions while, on the other hand, inappropriately arranged environments negatively affected children's behaviors and opportunities for social interaction.

By altering the classroom space, teachers can achieve learning goals as well as solve existing social and emotional issues. For example, Kritchevsky, Prescott, and Walling found that crowding caused by large pieces of play equipment and excessive furniture limited children's desire to freely move about the classroom. Cramped classrooms resulted in reduced cooperation and decreased collaborative play, which stymied children's engagement with learning materials. Eliminating unnecessary furniture and reducing the number of shelving units increased children's engagement with the physical environment and their positive relationships with others. This research revealed the importance of tailoring the classroom space to fit the needs, skill levels, and experiences of young children in early care and education programs.

"The classroom's physical design and décor are powerful nonverbal contributors to children's learning.

—Takiema Bunche Smith and Louise Ammentorp, "From Cinder Blocks to Building Blocks: Creating Beautiful Places in Children's Spaces"

Contemporary early childhood experts and researchers have confirmed the work of Kritchevsky, Prescott, and Walling. Ellen Nafe's research, for example, found a statistically significant correlation between children's positive behaviors and appropriately designed and arranged classrooms. Jim Greenman, author of *Caring Spaces, Learning Places,* declares that children deserve to spend their early years in environments purposefully designed to support their needs and stimulate learning. Other researchers, including Stephen Rushton and Elizabeth Larkin, assert that our most important priority must be to create classroom environments designed to foster meaningful communication and social connections, as these two factors are the true foundation of young children's learning. In *The Experience of Place,* author Tony Hiss says we all react, consciously and unconsciously, to the places in our lives. According to Hiss, the places where we spend our time have a profound impact on who we are as people and what we can become.

Because children spend an inordinate amount of time in early childhood classrooms, we must critically think about classroom design with a different viewpoint. Today, it is generally accepted that the arrangement of furniture and selection of learning materials within the classroom have a far-reaching influence on children's growth and development. Yet, we often find ourselves placing too much emphasis on what accreditation or licensing standards stipulate for furnishings and less emphasis on the more important variable of emotional or reflective effects of the classroom on young children.

Don Norman, a prominent academic in the field of cognitive science and design, coined the term reflective design. In his book *The Design of Everyday Things,* Norman describes three types of design:

- **Visceral:** how things look

- **Behavioral:** how people function within the design

- **Reflective:** the emotional impact of the design

Contemporary artist and expert designer of home interiors Susie Frazer uses this reflective methodology to design rooms in homes. She cultivates a sense of balance and calm in a room to support both children and adults to be their very best. She does this by infusing natural elements that activate well-being, such a tree twigs, live plants, neutral colors, and water effects. If we as early childhood practitioners are to follow the idea of reflective design, we must pay less attention to the furniture's functionality and more attention to how it is arranged and positioned in the classroom. In reflective design practice, it is also important to commit to designing classroom spaces that are aesthetically beautiful and have a positive emotional effect on young children.

2

Viewpoints: A Child's Perspective

Children Have a Unique Point of View

Young children view the world from a different perspective from adults. Children's unique perspectives are greatly determined by their height. They are built close to the ground, so they are always discovering close up: the small ant hill in the crack of the sidewalk, the tiny acorn peeking out from under a fallen leaf, or the glistening droplets on the dandelion.

Young Children are Egocentric

Young children naturally think about themselves, their own needs and views. They believe the world revolves around their perceptions and that everyone feels the same as they do. Because young children are so egocentric, they comprehend situations and events from the point of self. They find it difficult to see another's perspective; they struggle to realize that what they think is not necessarily what others think.

Young Children Do Not Extrapolate Meaning

Young children find it challenging to extrapolate meaning. They have limited capacity to make quantum leaps in their thinking. For example, in the fall teachers will hang leaves of different sizes, shapes, and colors from the ceiling—some low, some high. We expect children to make meaning of all these leaves hanging at different lengths in the classroom, but unless children are introduced to the experience of a tree in its autumn glory, the pretty leaves hanging from the classroom ceiling are nothing more than visual noise.

Young Children Have Myopic Vision

Young children see the world in a similar way to horses with blinders. Have you ever seen horse-drawn carriages in a city park with the horse's peripheral vision blocked by blinders? The blinders keep the horse from being distracted by what is going on around him. Young children view the world with myopic or binocular vision, seeing only what is immediately in front of them or directly below their feet.

▲ Adult view.

Children's Physical Perspectives Differ from Adults'

Take a closer look at the difference between an adult's visual perspective and a young child's. This image was taken from the adult's height. Look closely. What do you see? Your views of the classroom are, for the most part, dependent upon your height. From an adult perspective, you can easily see the learning materials on the shelves, the objects on top of the shelves, and other areas of the classroom.

▲ Child view.

Now take a look at the same spot in the classroom, this time from a child's perspective. Notice the difference. For a small child, views are dramatically different from the adult's. The child may see the learning materials on the shelves and a little of what resides on top of the shelves. For the most part, she cannot see over the shelves or see many other parts of the classroom, so that from this specific vantage point, she does not know what play opportunities are available. From a child's height and binocular viewpoint, her views are limited.

You may be asking yourself: Why should I be concerned about children's viewpoints? Why should I spend time and energy on changing or reorganizing my classroom to improve children's views? There are compelling benefits for doing so.

- **Eases transitions:** When the view from the doorway is engaging and welcoming, it encourages an easier transition for children. Johnna Darragh, professor of early childhood education, suggests the view from the entryway is an essential aspect of environmental design. Darragh suggests that entryways be thoughtfully designed in ways to support children's varied interests. For example, try placing activities at the classroom door, such as a lid game made from container tops and mounted on a small board, a bowlful of corks, or a variety of colorful sunglasses for children to try on and small nonbreakable mirrors where they can admire their reflections. The classroom environment should beckon the child in through the door.

▲ What fun to practice writing Chinese letters with chopsticks and making lovely designs in the sand!

▲ Offer authentic materials to explore on a curiosity table placed near the classroom entryway.

▲ Placing authentic objects, such as sand, plants, and tree cookies, near the classroom door sends a welcoming message inviting young children to come in and explore.

- **Expands views:** Improved views from the middle of the classroom help children see the room's potential and what opportunities are available to them.

- **Increases focus and engagement:** When children experience clear views of most of the classroom space from the entryway, they are immediately able to see its offerings. They walk readily through the classroom door and immediately become focused and engaged with the materials and space available to them because there are fewer visual distractions.

When Georgette, who enjoys nothing more than snuggling in with a book, can see the classroom's library from the door, she enters with much anticipation of the potential of a new book or possibly reading an all-time favorite for the umpteenth time. When Manuel crosses the classroom threshold, he can easily see his favorite activity—blocks. The children's views are calling them into the classroom, supporting their interests, and are unencumbered by furniture or the backs of cabinets. The views most important in an early childhood classroom are the view from the door, the view from the middle of the room, the view beneath the feet, and the view of the walls.

The View from the Classroom Door

Though we don't pay a great deal of attention to doors, they are an important part of our lives. Some doors elicit anxious feelings, such as the door to the dentist's office. Entering the door of your favorite restaurant, on the other hand, creates happy, mouth-watering sensations. Regardless of the situation, doors are important because they help transition us from one spot to another and can affect our emotional state.

The classroom door is one of the most significant doors in a young child's life. The classroom entryway is where a child's education begins—where motivation, curiosity, encouragement, engagement, learning, and new friendships commence. Because the classroom door plays such an important role of transitioning children from the outside world into the classroom world, critically examine the view from the door. Begin by standing directly in the middle of the entryway. Focus your eyes straight ahead. Look to your left, then to the right, and take note of what you see. Now, crouch down to the height of the children in the classroom. Repeat the process of looking around the room. What differences do you see at the adult height compared to the children's height? Most likely, your perspective as an adult is much different from the children's. As an adult, you have a wide-lens view of the entire classroom. A child's view, however, is quite myopic. Make your hands into binoculars and hold them up to your eyes. Go back to the classroom door, crouch down again, and look through your "binoculars." What do you see? That is pretty much what the children see upon entering the space. From this view you might see table legs, backs of cabinets, cots, children's cubbies, and more table legs.

Now reconsider your entryway from a child's perspective. Are there any inviting views for a young child? Is there a bounty of curiosities and surprises on the other side of your classroom door? Can the children see these curiosities upon entering the classroom?

When educators design and create enticing views from the doorway, children will be eager to cross the classroom threshold. For children to easily transition into the classroom, there must be a compelling reason to enter. The following are strategies, ideas, and things to avoid when creating wondrous views from the classroom doorway.

Create a Curiosity Table

Place a small table near the entryway to the classroom. Position the table so it is easily visible from the door. Children should have a clear view of its contents as they enter.

The curiosity table is an invitation to come in, to actively engage, to discover. The goal of the curiosity table is to provoke children's interest, to pique curiosity about the interesting objects placed there, and to ignite their minds and bodies so they are eager to make the transition into the classroom.

▲ Created from an old door, this curiosity table holds lots of amazing objects for children to discover.

Consider these tips to create your own curiosity table.

- Collect, arrange, and display materials in meaningful and purposeful ways. Do not burden the table with clutter; rather, select a few items to purposely position on the table. Artfully display the selected items by using easels, interesting containers, and trays.

- Intentionally select objects that would delight and spark children's curiosity. Seek out authentic objects, real rather than plastic. Providing authentic objects to explore and investigate enhances children's opportunities for meaningful experiences.

- Offer highly sensorial objects. It is widely accepted that children learn through hands-on, interactive experiences, so it is important for the curiosity table to offer objects that invite exploration. Offer items such as tree bark, natural sponges, driftwood, pussy-willow buds, and soft green moss.

▲ Provide a variety of highly sensorial and novel objects on curiosity table.

▲ Imagine a child's excitement over scrubbing flower petals into a fine dust with this screen and dish scrubber!

- Provide unique objects. Young children's attention spans are short; yet, when presented with something new or novel, research suggests that the brain becomes considerably more receptive and attentive. When the brain grows accustomed to a particular object, activity, or space, it has a tendency to tune out. People pay closer attention to ideas, information, and objects when they are new and different. The seminal research of neuroscientist Paul Silvia suggests that for materials to be interesting they must be novel. These objects can be those never encountered before or they can be familiar objects examined from a different perspective. Concurring with Paul Silvia, Australian researcher Kate Reid believes that while some objects may have decreased interest for children over periods of time, objects that are new and novel tend to consistently produce an increased interest. The experience of exploring a door handle, for instance, is a good example of this theory. Although most preschool children have often encountered and actually used a door handle, few children have encountered a doorknob without the actual door. Offering a doorknob (or perhaps many knobs) to manipulate provides children the opportunity to experience novel aspects of a familiar object.

"

Our experience also confirms that children need a great deal of freedom: the freedom to investigate and to try, to make mistakes, and to correct mistakes, to choose where and with whom to invest their curiosity, intelligence, and emotions. Children need freedom to appreciate the infinite resources of their hands, their eyes, and their ears, the resources of forms, materials, sounds, and colors. They need the freedom to realize how reason, thought, and imagination can create continuous interweavings of things and can move and shake the world.

—Loris Malaguzzi

Intriguing Objects for a Curiosity Table

- Kitchen whisk
- Tree pod
- Green onions with roots
- Handmade or crocheted doily
- Dried okra pod
- Variety of keys on ring
- Ornate serving spoon
- Driftwood
- Lacy ribbon
- Dandelions
- Wooden spoon
- Small hinge
- Natural sponge
- Small metal sieve
- Fresh herbs
- Empty thread spools
- Sea coral
- Rose petals
- Expired license plate
- Foreign coins and bills
- Snake skin
- Mounted butterfly

- Honeycomb
- Kaleidoscope
- Lotus seed pod
- Napkin ring
- Seashell
- Chestnut pod
- Wheat stalk
- Grass clump with roots and dirt
- Screw nuts and washers
- Seed heads
- Unique buttons
- Pinecone
- Japanese fan
- Fashion jewelry necklace
- String of beads
- Prickly cacti
- Sea glass
- Petrified wood
- Fossil
- View Master and slides
- Osage orange
- Camera

- Birchwood bark
- Doorknob
- Pastry brush
- Locust tree pod
- Periscope
- Moss on twig
- Caterpillar*
- Sunflower
- Pineapple top

*Show children how to gently hold the caterpillar, and be sure to return the caterpillar to the outdoors.

Safety note: Be aware of children's allergies and toxic materials. Do not include choking hazards on the curiosity table.

Offer natural elements. Young children are innately curious about the natural world. Natural objects are open-ended and wonderful to touch and manipulate. The number of natural objects you can easily collect for children's explorations is infinite. Just walk outside and see what you can find!

▲ Place a few objects to represent buildings and some empty spools of thread on a curiosity table.

▲ Exploring the textures of pods and seeds is an interesting experience for young children.

▲ Buttons and a tree cookie provided for classification experiences offer a wonderful sensory experience in a pre-K classroom.

Don't have an extra table or possibly the space to put another table by the door? Try placing other materials with high interest to both children and parents. Try floating wall shelves. A floating shelf, available at most home improvement stores, can be quickly and easily hung on a wall near the entryway. Try to find a shelf with a lip so the objects you place on it will stay put. Hang several floating shelves to display a variety of objects, including the following:

- Classroom scrapbook with pictures of children involved in daily experiences

- Children's artwork in a three-ring binder with plastic sleeves

- Framed pictures of children and their artwork

- A favorite storybook

- Daily classroom schedules in a frame

- Three-dimensional artwork created by the children. Change the display frequently to stimulate interest.

If you do not have a suitable table or enough space, try using a curiosity basket. A medium-sized basket with low sides works best because children can easily view its contents. To give the basket importance, place it on a small rug. Woven or braided rugs are more visually interesting, so they are a good option. Wooden placemats or thick table runners also work well. To avoid slippage, add a sticky mat under the placemat, table runner, or rug.

Judge how many objects to put in the curiosity basket based on the size of the objects. Remember, less is more. You want children to be intrigued and curious about the basket's contents. Putting too much stuff in the basket has a tendency to dilute young children's attention. To create a sense of wonder, do not include electronics or plastic items, only authentic or real objects. To find authentic objects, consider objects found in the kitchen, at the beach or park, the garage, or the garden.

Type of Curiosity Table	Focus	Examples
Nature	Observing	Seashells, rocks, leaves, flowers
Machines and Gears	Tinkering	Nuts and bolts, gears, old adding machines, typewriters
Loose Parts	Building	Spools, funnels, buttons
Cultural	Understanding	Cultural items from families
Community	Discovering	Artifacts from local businesses, such as a hardware store
Art Materials	Exploring	Clay, ribbon, pastels, beads
Tools and Gadgets	Investigating	Whisks, beaters, basters, kitchen scale

▲ A few seashells and some magnifying glasses make wonderful additions to the curiosity table.

▲ Snakeskins make for lively conversations and hands-on learning.

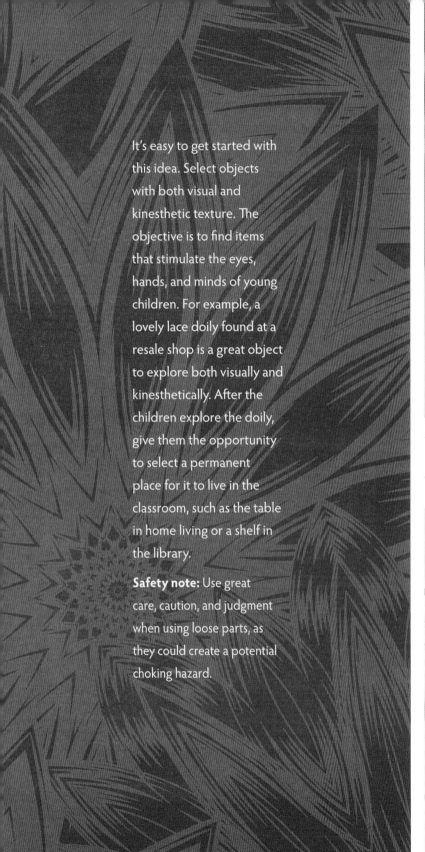

It's easy to get started with this idea. Select objects with both visual and kinesthetic texture. The objective is to find items that stimulate the eyes, hands, and minds of young children. For example, a lovely lace doily found at a resale shop is a great object to explore both visually and kinesthetically. After the children explore the doily, give them the opportunity to select a permanent place for it to live in the classroom, such as the table in home living or a shelf in the library.

Safety note: Use great care, caution, and judgment when using loose parts, as they could create a potential choking hazard.

▲ Place a pile of nuts and bolts on the curiosity table and watch creativity happen.

▼ Adding herbs to the curiosity table is a perfect incentive for children's tactile and olfactory experiences.

An estate sale provides the perfect opportunity to find unique silverware such as large serving spoons or soup ladles. Typically, old and inexpensive serving utensils have fascinating bumps and crevices to visually and kinesthetically explore.

A good resource for textured objects is a fabric store. Browse the remnant bin for small pieces of interesting fabric or ribbons with different textures and patterns such as furry items, or those with raised threads, bumps, or holes. You may want to ask families for fabric donations—just be sure to clearly communicate that you are looking for fabrics with texture.

Don't forget the sense of smell when selecting objects for the curiosity basket. Place a bouquet of fresh mint in the basket, or pull some basil (roots and all) from the garden and place it in a low container. Pluck from the garden or purchase some fresh rosemary or lavender, and then place it in a mound of clay. Sometimes you can find rosemary or mint growing by the roadside. Be aware of any allergies or other considerations when choosing scented materials.

Make friends with your local florists. They often have bits and pieces of flowers, stems, petals, and ribbons left over from making floral arrangements, which would typically be thrown out. These floral remnants make wonderful additions to the curiosity table or basket.

For a change of pace, use a box with a lid for the objects. Children always enjoy an element of mystery and surprise; they will look forward to coming into the classroom just to see what special object is under the lid.

The curiosity table or basket invites children to investigate using all their senses, which promotes critical thinking and wonder. A table filled with curious objects encourages exploration, discovery, and an examination of a variety of wondrous objects that can be found nearby. Continually be on the lookout for objects you can add to the table.

▲ Make a curiosity table out of a large tree cookie. Just add legs (purchased at the neighborhood home improvement store) and presto, a beautiful table.

If you don't have an available table or basket, trying using the floor for a curiosity space. Define an area on the floor with a small rug and place interesting objects in a gift box. Place an acrylic mirror on the rug for added dimension or perhaps a few battery-powered lights.

Create a Curiosity Mat for Infants

Curiosity is a universal characteristic for young children, even infants. Give babies plenty of opportunities for exploration by creating a curiosity mat filled with interesting objects to see, feel, and taste. Because infants learn by mouthing objects, it is important to offer items that can be sanitized (including the mat). Use authentic materials rather than a plastic toy from the room's shelf. **Safety note:** Be sure the objects are large enough not to be choking hazards. Ideas for mats include wooden placemats, small bath rugs, or shower mats. Items of curiosity from the kitchen, for example, could include a small metal whisk, plastic pastry brush, and metal colander.

Case Study #1, View from the Door: Before

When family members and children walked into the room prior to the redesign, they could see a table, black chairs, and a shelving unit directly in front of them. The table and chairs, however, were partially obscuring the objects on the white shelf. The wonderful cozy couch on the back wall by the windows was completely hidden from view.

- Child's perspective is table legs

- Child's view to popular areas is semi-blocked

- No space designed for transition from outside world to inside world of classroom

- Portfolios not being reviewed by family members

- Focal point is missing

- Three separate large objects hanging from ceiling

- Wastebasket is front and center

▲ Before

After

The table and black chairs were moved to the left side of the classroom, and the couch was moved front and forward, along with an ottoman found in the center's storage room. Book buckets filled with interesting storybooks were added to the space. Out of view to the right are wall shelves containing children's portfolios, easily accessible to both family members and children. Teachers report that the portfolios are enjoyed more frequently since the classroom's transformation. Because this is a younger-age classroom, family members enjoy the convenience of sitting on the ottoman when helping their children take off their coats and getting one last hug. Also out of view and to the immediate left is the block area, a favorite of children in this classroom. With the new classroom design, children can see this block area as soon as they enter the classroom.

- The couch was moved to the front of the classroom, creating a cozy space for both children and their family members. The teacher reported improved family involvement with children's portfolios.

- The tree limb surrounded by twinkle lights hung over the block corner and visible from the door creates an easier transition into classroom.

- The curtain creates a softness and is also an ideal spot for alone time.

- Table legs have been moved to the side and are partially out of view.

▲ After

Case Study #2, View from the Door: Before

The entryway of the preschool classroom had cubbies on all three sides, so when children entered the classroom there was no visual interest or attraction until they walked many feet in and turned to their right. The cubbies on the left and front were against two walls. The cubby on the right was positioned perpendicular to the doorway. The cubby to the right of the door completely blocked the children's vision into the classroom. Furthermore, once children walked several feet into the classroom past the cubby on the right and turned right into the main part of the classroom, they would see the cramped home living area, the science corner, and a light table tucked behind the shelf. Once children got past the cubbies, they were still unable to completely see the exciting opportunities in the science corner.

- Three sets of cubbies blocked children's view of the classroom.

- Once children walked past the cubby on the right and turned to the right, they saw a confined home living space and partially saw the light table in the science corner located behind the home living area.

- The view from the door was custodial, so children could not see the fun opportunities available to them. This made the transition from outside world into classroom challenging.

▲ Before

▲ Before

After

The cubby positioned immediately to the right of the classroom door was eliminated because it was not being used for children's belongings and the number of students did not justify three cubby units. Once this visual obstacle was removed, the classroom opened up. When children walk into the classroom, they immediately see the home living area because the unneeded cubby is not blocking their view.

- The cubby blocking children's view was not needed so it was removed from the classroom, which resulted in opening the viewpoint from the door.

- The science area was moved to another part of the classroom by the large windows, allowing the home living area space to increase in size.

- Cabinets were moved to the side of the center so the view from the door is transparent and center is easily visible.

▲ After

- Because the home living area was popular with the children in this classroom, more square footage was devoted to the space. The front of the area was left open (with no visual or physical barriers), so children were excited to come into the classroom and begin playing.

- Eliminating the entryway cubby and opening the face of the home living center made a dramatic change with the added natural light.

- The beautiful windows, which were hardly noticeable in the before image, now provide a place for scientific investigation.

- The face of the home living area is open. The shelving unit is positioned so children can easily see the cabinet's contents. The cabinet backs are no longer blocking children's views. Pulling out the shelving units from the wall near the window created another entryway into the home living area, reducing the potential for traffic jams.

- There is a makeshift side table between the two blue chairs that was created by turning a wooden basket upside down. This extra table creates an added area of interest and a place for children to gather.

- The table is set and ready for dramatic play. When children finish their time in this area, they return the table to its original setup. This promotes a shared responsibility for the area's housekeeping maintenance. The wooden chairs by the table and the two blue living room chairs are positioned at an angle, which sends a message of welcome to children.

▲ After

More Strategies for Inviting Entrances

Position Cabinets Face Forward

To create better views from the classroom door, try positioning as many cabinets facing forward as you can—the cabinets' shelves should be in the children's line of sight. When the fronts of the cabinets are visible, children can easily see what's on the shelves, and there is more enticement to enter the classroom.

In this image, you see the backs of three cabinets from the classroom doorway. Even though the teacher has decorated the cabinet backs with posters, there are no visual clues as to what these cabinets hold and whether, in fact, their contents would be interesting to a preschooler.

Cluster Tables Away from the Classroom Door

Early childhood teachers typically position larger-sized tables on the tile flooring because these tables are often used for mealtime and art activities, and the tile flooring makes for easy cleanup. For the most part, classroom entryways use tile flooring to reduce the likelihood of tracking dirt onto carpet. So it seems sensible to place larger-sized tables on the tile floor near the doorway; however, clumping tables near the entryway creates a feeling of institutional living that does not send positive messages to children or their family members.

▲ Avoid positioning cabinet backs to face the entryway.

▲ Avoid clustering tables near the entry of the classroom.

Another problem with clustering tables at the entryway is that all the children see upon entering the classroom are a multitude of table legs and a sea of tabletops, which are not that exciting or interesting. There is nothing about the view that welcomes children or makes them want to transition from their world to your world. The classroom doorway should send a message of welcome: Come on in. This is the place for you. This is the place that you absolutely want to be.

So what do you do when the availability of tiled space is limited and you still need to position tables on a washable surface? Determine the number of children's seats (and accompanying adult seats) required at the highest time of need, probably during lunch or snack time. Once you know the number, look at the total number of spaces available at the required tables. You may find it possible to arrange tables in such a way as to reduce the table-leg effect. For example, put two rectangular tables together to make a square or family-style configuration. Or, perhaps position two tables into a *T* or *L* configuration or put three tables in an *H*, *I*, or possibly a *Z* configuration. Experiment to find what works best for you.

▲ Avoid placing tables in rows.

Separate Tables with Shelving Units

To reduce the overall clutter of table legs, try separating the tables with small shelving units, or if you have the room, place two shelving units back to back. This configuration allows each shelf to serve two separate tables. Use one table, for example, as a manipulative table (with adjoining shelf) that doubles as a meal table. Use the second table for art activities (with adjoining shelf) that doubles as another meal table.

Camouflage Tables with Homelike Furniture

Is there a way to camouflage the tables by using a piece of equipment that is less institutional and more personal for young children? For example, perhaps you have the room to place a shelving unit facing the interior of the classroom directly across from the classroom door. Because you don't want to have the back of the cabinet facing the children, you could put the curiosity table with two chairs bumped up against the back. Or, maybe a small—but sturdy—bench could be placed against the cabinet's backside. Add a few pillows and a basket of books, and you will have a perfect place for children (and family members) to sit and chat upon arriving into the classroom. This is also an effective technique for helping children transition from the outside to the inside. Most importantly, the table legs are hidden, creating a more personal and comfortable place for children (and adults) to learn.

In this classroom entryway, a comfy couch was placed on an eye-catching rug, which were positioned at an angle. Even though the couch is not camouflaging table or chair legs, your eyes are drawn to this cozy setting. Children enjoy cozying up, reading a book, and using the area for chatting with family members and teachers. Just by moving the tree cookie table to the side of the rug, this area is perfect for group meetings.

Create a Comfy Place

Whether or not you are camouflaging a shelf or tables, a small couch or bench designed for sitting and chatting can help to ease a child's transition at the beginning of the day. Children, as well as family members, may need extra snuggles and hugs before separating. A sitting space can also be used for end-of-day rituals, such as looking at a child's portfolio or reading a short storybook. These routines may be important for some families.

Don't have a comfy couch available? There are other ways to create a cozy space. Here are some alternatives.

- Beanbag
- Bench
- Ottoman
- Tree stump
- Padded chair

- Rocker with pillow
- Futon
- Crate with cushion
- Chaise lounge
- Cushy Pillows, Rug

Don't have enough space for an extra piece of furniture by the classroom entryway? Try a welcome easel. Display welcoming messages or information about the day's events on the easel. You may want to include images of the children playing in the classroom. Place the easel near the door so families can see it when entering and exiting. As with the curiosity table, be sure to keep the information and images on the easel fresh and current. No autumn leaves when it is snowing outside!

Avoid Custodial Furniture

The way both family members and children feel when they enter the classroom, in large part, has to do with how the classroom is arranged. The sight of custodial furniture, such as cubbies or changing tables, does not induce much excitement. Children would be excited, however, if the sensory table filled with interesting pieces of driftwood, sand, and small twigs is placed near the classroom entry—now that looks like lots of fun!

Many classrooms have a place where families sign their child in at morning time and out at the end of the day; this is a custodial task. Typically, sign-in and -out boards are placed on some type of shelf close to the classroom door for parent convenience. Sometimes, however, it is too convenient; for example, we have all seen the parent who signs her child out quickly. She opens the classroom door, props the door open with her body, signs out her child, and calls for the child to hurry and get ready to leave. You barely have time to say hello before they are both out the door and gone. There's no time for conversation, no time for saying goodbye, and certainly no time for mom to have a look around the classroom to see that exciting stuff is going on. More importantly, her child has no moments of explanation about the day and no time for storytelling or sharing the day's accomplishments. To encourage family members to linger, consider moving the sign-in and -out area to the middle or even the back of the room. The parent, then, will be forced to walk through the room. Perhaps during this walk, she will see and hear about her child's amazing day.

Avoid Tall Furniture

Positioning tall furniture near the entryway obstructs children's view into the classroom. If children cannot see at least part of the classroom's interior and its offerings, there is no reason to come inside. Learning centers boxed in with high shelves or furniture are not welcoming to children. The classroom, especially at the entryway, should provide complete transparency and positive views for young children. To help create transparency at the classroom entryway, a rule of thumb is to place the shortest pieces of furniture in the middle of the classroom, taller furniture on the outer perimeters of the classroom, and the tallest pieces of furniture against the walls.

▲ Taken from the classroom doorway from the child's viewpoint, this image illustrates how tall furniture obstructs young children's views.

▲ Avoid classroom walkways that take up valuable square footage and significantly reduce usable space for children.

Avoid Creating Walkways

Early childhood teachers tend to create walkways when they arrange furniture, but in so doing they inadvertently block children's views. By definition, walkways are passageways created to transition a person from one area to another. Early childhood classrooms do not need passages devoted only to walking. Rather, classrooms need areas designed for young children's activity and engagement. Walkways take up valuable square footage and can significantly reduce the amount of usable space for children. Look around your classroom, particularly from the doorway. Have you inadvertently designed walkways that obstruct the view? Are there areas used for walking and nothing else? If so, try to eliminate walkways or fuse them into a learning center and turn wasted space into a hub of action.

At this classroom's doorway, there are cubbies on the left and a wall of cabinet-like equipment on the right, creating a walkway entry into the space. Behind the desk and shelving unit on the right is the block area, a favorite destination place for the preschoolers in the classroom. To gain physical and visual access to the fun block area, children must go down the walkway, turn right, and make another right turn to finally be in the block center. The walkway is dull and lacks excitement; it also consumes forty feet of valuable space, making it unavailable for children's activities and experiences.

To eliminate the walkway, the cubbies were moved to the far back left side of the classroom, the shelving and desk were removed from the classroom because they were unneeded, the block corner was repositioned to the far back right side of the classroom, and the newly created space was used for a larger home living area (another favorite of the preschoolers) and art center.

The most important job of the classroom door is to help children transition from their outside worlds into your classroom. A welcoming transition area affects the behavior and actions of young children, and this space should be inviting to family members as well. Begin thinking about the entryway as a teaching and learning tool rather than just a means of ingress and egress.

Infants and Transitioning into the Classroom

For an infant, the view from the door isn't as important as it is for a preschooler. Does this mean the view from the door for this age group isn't important? Absolutely not! Although less important to the infant, the entryway is critically important to the infant's parent or caregiver coming into the classroom. The view from here can send positive or negative messages, and we have only a few precious seconds to send positive messages to those coming through the infant doorway.

When selecting a place for infant care, most families agree that a safe and nurturing environment is high on the list of requirements. According to author and educator Jim Greenman, parents use words such as "loving caregivers," "safe places," and "homelike environments" when describing the perfect place for their babies. Indeed, most families want a home away from home, a place where there is a sense of security, coziness, and warmth. As author and family care expert Linda Armstrong asserts, "The term *home* means more than physical space; home is a feeling that comes over us when we think about being inside with people we love."

To develop a welcoming atmosphere in the infant classroom, try creating a more homelike, or what Armstrong calls "homestyle," child care environment. Use the following ideas to get you started.

Declutter

Some classrooms have built-in cubbies near the door, so moving the custodial cubbies to another part of the room is not feasible. If this is the case with your infant room, try adding a lamp, framed family photographs, landscape pictures, a textured table runner, or water elements to the top of the cubbies. To maintain a positive welcoming message to families, it is important to keep this area free from classroom clutter.

Add Seating

Position a rocking or other type of chair or a bench near the door for both caregivers and family members to use. It's a perfect place for one last hug from mommy, daddy, grandmother, or any other caregiver.

Infuse Lighting

Add ambient lighting near the doorway. Placing a small table lamp on top of the infants' cubbies adds softness and a look of home. If you are concerned about it tipping, select a wide-based lamp and either screw it to the cubby top or use heavy duty double-sided Velcro to secure it. Don't have an outlet near the door? Search online for a battery-powered LED lamp. The lithium battery is rechargeable and lasts up to ten hours, so you don't have to continually purchase new batteries. Some lamps have speakers powered by Bluetooth and are also compatible with cell phones and computers. Some LED lamps are dimmable and have different colored lights depending on the mood you want to create in the room.

Add Soft Sounds

Small table water fountains create a relaxing sound. If you are unable to have a water fountain, try playing some sounds of cascading water from a CD, through a computer, or on your smartphone.

Add Nature Art

Look for a landscape painting at a garage sale or local recycle shop. Choose images of flowers, trees, mountains, rivers, or any type of nature scene. Place the framed picture near the doorway on the wall next to the table lamp, framed family pictures, or water element.

The View from the Middle of the Classroom

Another important view for young children is the view from the middle of the room. Imagine yourself in the middle of your classroom. Get down to the height of the children you serve. Look in all four directions and observe the surroundings. If you cannot easily see into the majority of the areas from the middle of the classroom, it is time to rearrange the furniture to improve children's views.

▲ Too many shelving units obstruct children's views, reduce foot space, and create confining spaces.

To improve children's views, the space needs to be quite transparent. *Transparency* in classroom design means children have a clear line of sight into the learning center or area before they actually get into it. Creating transparency helps children to see the potential and excitement of the area and increases engagement. When children are able to see into learning centers and around the spaces, they are better able to see what materials are available to them, plan their courses of play, and have the room (or foot space) to execute their plans. There are several simple and easy strategies for creating classroom transparency.

Reduce Shelving Units

Too much furniture in an early childhood classroom is the biggest barrier to transparency. In the above image, there are four learning areas defined by seven or possibly eight shelving units. Because of all the furniture, you cannot see the purpose of any of these areas. Are these four areas designed to be a block corner, science area, home living space, or something else? If you cannot tell from your viewpoint, neither can the children.

Position Cabinets to Face Forward

Cabinets that face forward entice children to come into the learning center. In the classroom photo on page 50, two cabinet backs face the children's line of view from the doorway so that children cannot see their contents. The two cabinets are at different heights with different backs. From a design standpoint, it would be better to have two identical shelves for visual continuity. This could easily be accomplished because the shelf facing the tile is identical to the left shelf with its back facing the camera. Put like sized cabinets together. Better still is to position the cabinets face forward so children can see their contents from the door or from the middle of the room. You might also place the cabinets back to back, so one cabinet faces the interior of the room and one faces the exterior. Doubling up cabinets also creates more places for children to enter and exit the area.

Increase Foot Space

Another reason for reducing the number of shelving units is to increase children's foot space. Shelving units take up valuable square footage, so too many shelves result in a reduced amount of available space for children to use. When there is more space for children to navigate their bodies, there is less opportunity for them to accidentally bump into each other or to inadvertently knock over another child's construction.

> Reduced Shelf Space =
> Increased Foot Space

Define Spaces with Fabric

One way to achieve transparency is to define spaces with something other than shelving units. Could you, for example, define the space with something hanging from the ceiling as the above image illustrates? To set apart this home living space, the teacher simply used three curtain rods, looped thin curtains over the rods, and hung them from the ceiling with fishing line. In place of curtain rods, you could use bamboo sticks purchased at a local craft store or long sticks deposited on the ground after a windstorm.

Notice that the home living space on page 51 offers several ways to get into the space so children can easily enter and exit the area; this prevents traffic congestion. Also note that the face of the space is open and transparent. The image to the left illustrates this design idea. The teacher designed a welcome table with framed family pictures immediately inside the classroom door. Because this is a very tiny space, the small area rug perfectly defines the space, and there is no need for large cumbersome shelves.

Define Spaces with Rugs

Typically, teachers create their spaces by using cabinets to surround the space they wish to define. Rather than using multiple cabinets, try using a rug to define a learning center. This block center is located immediately across from the classroom door. The area is defined by two shelving units but is open to the children when they enter the classroom. Notice the construction table in the middle of the rug. Under the table is a wicker basket filled with farm objects, which is the children's current interest as they recently visited a horse stable on a neighborhood excursion. Because the construction table is lightweight and small, it can be easily moved to the side when children's block constructions require extra space.

Case Study #3, View from the Door: Before

On the rug area, there are four different learning centers including the popular home living and block areas. It looks like there are ten separate shelving units (perhaps more) in this area. When children walk into the classroom, they see the backs of these cabinets.

Critically think about each shelving unit in the classroom, and ask yourself the following questions:

- Why is it in the classroom? What is its purpose? Is it absolutely necessary? Is it in the best position?

- Are there any shelving units blocking children's views? If there are, consider ways to reposition these shelves. Could you eliminate a shelf?

- From a child's view, do you see the backs of the shelves? If so, how could you reposition so the shelves' contents are visible? Could the shelves be positioned so just the ends are exposed?

▲ Before

After

Several shelves were eliminated, and the front side of the center was made transparent so children could see into the space before they actually made their way into the home living center. Children can see the manipulative center, which is anchored by a rug instead of shelving units. Behind the manipulative center is the block area, which has its open face to the tile so children can see into the center from that direction.

▲ After

▲ After

Case Study #4, View from the Door: Before

Most of the fun stuff is going on behind the two shelves located in the middle of the room facing the tables. Although children can see the contents of these shelves because they are positioned forward, they cannot see what is behind the two shelving units. Hidden from view are the library, manipulative, home living, and block areas. There is little to invite children into the room.

Additionally, the view is visually cluttered. Notice all the stuff on top of the cabinets, the box filled with baby dolls on the back wall, and the pillows stacked high in the corner of the room. Young children do not have the capacity to filter out all this visual stimuli and will become overwhelmed trying to extrapolate meaning from their cluttered classroom. We will discuss reducing clutter in more depth in chapter 5.

This image shows a partial view from behind the shelving units. Notice the far back corner, which is a library area. Because the space is surrounded by a shelving unit and cubbies and the entryway is small, it is difficult for children to see the contents of this area. Although they can see the pillows, the children could not retrieve them on their own because of the height of the shelves where they are stored. The comfortable padded chair with the pillow is located outside the quiet area, so its purpose as a reading chair is minimized. It is not hard to understand why the teacher said this area was rarely used. Note the gray and white rug in the far back corner; it is beautiful but hidden by the classroom's furniture. The rug is also too big for the space.

▲ Before

▲ Before

After

The once obscured quiet corner has been redesigned and repurposed. The positioning of the furniture makes the space open, warm, and inviting. It is no longer designated as the quiet corner, but is now the living room adjacent to the home living area. In addition to the cozy chair previously located outside the area, an identical chair was added from another part of the classroom. Many reading materials such as books and magazines have been added to the space. Rather than the tall shelving units blocking children's views, the area is now defined by a textured rug that was found in the center's storage closet. Notice the large entry area, which allows children to see into the center as well as easily enter and exit the area. The cozy rug invites children to sit, and the furniture positioning sends a welcome message for them to enter the space. The white book shelf is actually a tall cabinet turned on its side. Its footprint is much smaller than a regular bookcase, so it takes up less room and gives children more foot space. Personalizing the area with children's pictures, a live plant, soft pillows, and a child's framed artwork entices children to sit down and enjoy conversation or a book.

Remember the two shelves in the middle of the room that were blocking children's viewpoints to all the fun centers located on the rug? They were removed from the middle of the room and placed so that the face of the home living center is in clear view. Children can see all the wonderful possibilities for play. The large rug that was hidden in the back corner has been moved front and forward, and it is now being used to anchor the home living area. Reducing the number of shelving units and using the rug to define the home living center opens the children's views.

All the furniture and rugs were found in the classroom or center's storage room. Nothing was purchased for this classroom transformation. Here are some lessons we can learn from this example.

- The shelving units were in the middle of the room facing forward. Even though the children could see the shelves' contents, the cabinets were still obscuring children's viewpoints. They could not see the potential of many of the classroom's areas.

- Because the face of the home living center is now open and transparent, there are many ways to enter and exit this area.

- Much of the clutter on the top of the shelves has been removed, so children do not have to filter through the visual noise.

▲ After

▲ After

Case Study #5, View from the Door: Before

A visitor to this classroom sees a large pillar and the backs of shelving units for the block center. There is nothing of interest to draw children into the classroom.

Because of the way the shelves are positioned, the open space at the bottom right is wasted. Its only purpose is a walkway used to enter the classroom. Most early childhood classrooms are small, so every inch is important. Take note of the windows in the upper left corner of the image. They are hidden by the shelving units but will take on greater importance, as you will see, in the after images.

▲ Before

After

The block shelves were removed, so they are no longer visual barriers. The block center was repositioned to the back corner of the room to the right of the windows. Repositioning the block center opened up the entire classroom and gave transparency to many of the centers. The pillar became an anchor for the home living area, transforming it from an obstacle to work around (or even ignore) to a seamless part of the center's design. The home living area is now the focal point as children enter the classroom.

Notice how the sink and stove were placed at an angle to soften the classroom's look and also to welcome children into the area. Hanging a picture on the pillar and placing a green plant on top of the refrigerator gives authenticity to the space and creates a homelike environment.

The wonderful floor-to-ceiling windows were hardly noticeable from the entryway because they were obscured by the block shelves. Now, natural light flows throughout the entire room. There is no longer a walkway as you enter the classroom, so there is no wasted space. Children are using every square inch available to them.

The block corner was relocated from the front of the room to the back corner. Note the openness of the center—there is more than one way to come into and exit the space. If children's block constructions become elaborate, it is easy to move the woodworking table in to expand the building area. The entire block center is positioned on an angle to the corner, and the shelving units are placed at the same angle as the rug. Areas positioned at an angle create more open spaces and are more visually welcome.

▲ After

▲ After

Rethinking Infant Space

Normally, infant rooms do not have an overabundance of shelves. What infant rooms do have, however, is an abundance of other equipment that takes up space: rocking chairs, cribs, changing tables, child-size tables and chairs, mats and crawling apparatus, and high chairs. Some rooms also contain what infant-toddler specialist Alycia Dotseth-Hall calls "baby containers," including baby swings, bouncy seats, and walkers. All this paraphernalia occupies valuable square footage.

You may be thinking that infants do not need foot space, so what's the problem? Although infants do not need foot space, they do need tummy space. One way to find space for tummy time is to eliminate the room's baby containers. Not only is there more space for tummy time, but the research work of John Persing and colleagues determined that these baby containers can be detrimental for children's growth and development. Early childhood development expert and author Heidi Murkoff recommends that caregivers encourage prone positioning and limit container time, or the time spent in bouncy seats and similar equipment. Make space for babies' tummies!

The View beneath the Feet

When we are unfamiliar with the landscape or unsure of our footing, we watch our step because we don't want to trip, stumble, or—worst-case scenario—fall. The view beneath our feet informs how we navigate the space. Likewise, the view beneath children's feet sends important messages about how to move about the classroom environment.

So, what is the view beneath children's feet? There are many views from the floor that send messages of how and where to move about the classroom. These views include created pathways through the classroom. Formed by cabinets and furniture, these pathways help inform children which direction to walk and how to move about the space. Important visual clues are also conveyed to children through floor coverings. A classroom's typical floor covering includes a combination of tile and carpet. In some classrooms, area rugs are scattered throughout the space. Varied floor coverings can create pathways and define spaces within the classroom. Because area rugs play a critical role in defining spaces and determining how children navigate the classroom, it is important to know about the purpose of rugs, their selection, and the placement of rugs in the classroom.

Area Rugs in the Classroom

It is common for a classroom to have at least one area rug—or perhaps more—in the environment. It is also common that, while some early childhood practitioners recognize their importance, many teachers give minimal thought to the three purposes of area rugs in the classroom. To be effective, all classroom rugs should fulfill at least one of the following functions:

- Defining or delineating a space
- Anchoring a piece of furniture
- Providing comfort

▲ The purpose of this rug is to define the quiet area, but its size and design do not create a sense of coziness.

▲ The purpose of this rug is to define a quiet and cozy space, which is accomplished through the rug's size, shape, and soft texture.

▲ The materials are hard to see when placed on top of a visually busy rug.

▲ The materials are much easier to see and distinguish when placed on a plain surface.

When selecting an area rug, consider the rug size, design, shape, and its placement within the classroom. Because the primary role of an area rug is to define a space, placing a rug that is either too big or too small sends confusing visual cues to young children. Like Goldilocks and the three bears, the rug size has to be just right. If the purpose of the space is to be a quiet and cozy area for reading, then the size of the rug should be smaller to send a message that the space is for sitting down and quietly reading or looking through a storybook. A large rug with a bright pattern and colors, on the other hand, sends a message for children to be active. While being active is a child's primary job in life, promoting lively movement in an area designed for quiet reading is not ideal.

A general rule of thumb is to purposefully select rugs that align with a specific center. Rugs with patterns or designs are appropriate for the home living area. Rugs with geometric designs, floral patterns, or oriental patterns placed in the kitchen area create a homey atmosphere. In the science area, natural rugs made of bamboo or those with botanical themes such as leaves, trees, or flowers make good choices.

Patterned rugs may interfere with children's constructions and creativity. A rug with a road imprinted on it, for example, may send a message to a child that all that should be done on this rug is to drive cars on the road. Busily patterned rugs may interfere with children's view. For example, it is easier to see the items on the construction table when they are placed on the plain surface on the right, which has no patterns.

For the block corner, select a plain rug with a low pile so children can easily construct tall towers and buildings without the chance of their structures wobbling and falling down because of the unevenness of the rug.

The following guidelines should be used when determining the appropriate rug shape.

- Rectangular rugs should be used in corners.

- Use rectangular rugs under square or rectangular tables.

- Place circular rugs under circular tables.

- Rectangular rugs work best in front of shelving units or cabinets with the rug's long side placed parallel to the cabinet face or shelves.

There are several visual design tricks to use when placing area rugs in the classroom. Teachers have a tendency to place area rugs in a corner with two sides jammed against two walls. Pulling out the area rug about one or two feet on both sides creates a visual openness. Creating space between the wall and the area rug helps children to visually understand where the learning center begins and ends.

Rather than placing the furniture directly on the area rug, try positioning pieces off the rug with a one- or two-foot gap between the rug's edge and the furniture piece. Making a gap between the rug's edge and furniture creates a visual openness and may offer another entryway into the area. Positioning a rectangular rug at an angle from a corner is a good way to make the space appear larger. Just be sure that the furniture around and off the rug is placed at the same angle.

Rugs are an important part of classroom design. They provide important visual cues and send messages regarding how to navigate the classroom. The next time you are in need of a new classroom rug, consider looking in a resale store, garage sale, or home decorator store for one that will fit your requirements.

Design Tips for Creating Views of Wonder

- Place a curiosity table near the doorway filled with interesting artifacts to pique children's attention.

- Position shelving at children's line of sight so that they can see what is on the shelves when entering the room.

- Eliminate shelving units (or visual obstacles) from the face of learning centers so their contents are clearly visible.

- Position the tallest furniture to the outside perimeter of the room so children can easily see into the room.

- Reduce shelving units to create more foot space and increase children's visibility.

- Use rugs instead of shelves to anchor centers for improved visibility.

- Create more than one entry or exit into each learning area to ease traffic congestion and improve views into the centers.

3

Furniture and Equipment Arrangement:
Balancing the Classroom Canoe

Finding Balance

Balance is everywhere. There's balance in architecture, mathematic equations, and even in a car's tires. There is also balance in nature. The ancient Greeks found beauty in what they called the *golden mean*, the idea of nothing in excess—neither too much nor too little. In science, a similar idea, the golden ratio, occurs over and over again in the natural world. Not only does it occur in human bodies and faces but also in the curvature of seashells, cloud formations, and even in the circular pattern of our universe. When the ratio of proportions is balanced, it is easier for our brains to process information.

Balancing the Classroom Canoe

Getting into a canoe can be tricky. You want to carefully climb in without tipping it over. Start by bending your knees and grabbing onto the side of the canoe closest to you. From there you will want to place one of your legs into the center of the canoe and grab onto the far side with your other hand. Then slowly bring your other leg into the canoe, and sit on the bench in the middle once you feel balanced. Yes, getting into a canoe requires thought, planning, and balance.

Designing a classroom can be a lot like getting in a canoe. Balanced classrooms prevent issues such as children running into each other, accidentally bumping into an amazing block tower and knocking it to the ground, or too many children confined to a small space—resulting in tussles and arguments. Unbalanced classrooms are environments with underused spaces, poor traffic flow, excessive furniture, and inefficient placement and positioning of equipment. The results can be unpleasant to both children and teachers. The solution to an unbalanced classroom is to reconfigure it with the balance of two areas in mind: furniture and equipment placement and furniture and equipment usage.

Balance of Furniture

Imagine your classroom is a canoe and you, of course, are the canoe's captain. Your responsibility is to steer the canoe from the helm located in the middle of the boat. Stand in the middle of your classroom and imagine the classroom divided into four quadrants: top left, top right, bottom left, and bottom right. Mentally picture putting the furniture and equipment located in your classroom's top left quadrant into the top left quadrant of your canoe. Next, picture putting the furniture and equipment located in the classroom's top right quadrant into your canoe's top right quadrant. Continue this mental exercise until all the classroom furniture is in the canoe.

What's happening to the balance of the canoe? Do you have more furniture in the bow (front) of your boat or the stern (back)? Is there more furniture on the port (left) side of the canoe than on the starboard (right) side? Because of the number of pieces of furniture and equipment on the right side of the canoe, is the boat tipping to the right? Will it soon capsize? The canoe may not be balanced. One potential reason for this imbalance is because teachers often position the home living area and block corner next to each other—typically in the same quadrant. The two centers often have a great deal of furniture. The home living area, for example, usually has a refrigerator, stove, sink, pantry, dress-up materials, dining table and chairs, ironing board, and so on. The block corner usually has several shelves for the blocks and other related items, such as trucks, cars, and road signs for children's construction and block play.

It is not enough to just balance the pieces of furniture in the classroom. There is onemore important piece to this design puzzle—the children's usage of the furniture and equipment.

Balance of Children's Usage of Furniture

A well-balanced classroom is one in which both the furniture and the children's usage of it are similar in all four quadrants. The home living and block centers are typically very popular areas. If these areas are both located in the top right quadrant of the classroom, not only is there a great deal of furniture in this space, but there is a great number of children using the furniture. This translates into reduced foot space, limited room to move about, and minimal space to play. It is easy to understand why squabbles and negative behaviors would occur in these areas.

Balance of furniture and equipment usage among the four quadrants is just as important as the balance of furniture placement. Once again—this time during independent play time—stand in the middle of the classroom and imagine it as a canoe. Note the location of all the children. Are there more in front or behind you? Are there more to the left or to the right? Do this several times throughout the day and over the course of the week, and then consider these questions: If your classroom were a canoe, would it tip to one side? Would it be off balance? If you answered yes to any or all of these questions, your classroom canoe might be unbalanced.

Is Your Classroom Balanced?	Yes	No
Are physical obstacles, such as shelving units, completely surrounding the learning center?		
Is there only one way in or out of a learning center that would disrupt children's ability to easily navigate the classroom?		
Is there a purpose for every piece of furniture and shelving unit in the classroom?		
Do any of the centers feel crowded?		
Are there specific areas in the classroom where negative behaviors occur more frequently?		
Are there dead spaces in the classroom, such as walkways that are taking up valuable space, which children could use more effectively?		
Is there more than one popular center in the same quadrant of the classroom?		
Is the group-time area used only during group time?		

Strategies for Balancing the Classroom Canoe

Proponents of the Chinese practice of *feng shui* understand the important link between our internal feelings or states of being and our external environments. The author of *Feng Shui for the Classroom*, Renee Heiss, suggests that harmony, flow, and balance are essential components of a positive classroom atmosphere, and all three are needed to create the optimum learning environment for young children. Try the following ideas to balance the feng shui of your classroom.

- As much as possible, position equal amounts of furniture (or centers) in all four quadrants of the classroom.

- Consider children's usage of the furniture in each quadrant to be sure usage is equally distributed throughout the classroom.

- Do not position two highly popular areas in the same quadrant—especially centers with lots of furniture.

- If possible, position the two most popular centers (or high-usage areas) in opposite quadrants, such as the top left and bottom right quadrant.

- Do not design areas that are only used for a small amount of time during the day. For example, the area designated for group time should also be used for other activities, such as the block center. Or the tables used for eating could also be designated as tables for manipulatives.

Consider each piece of furniture in the classroom to determine whether it is necessary. Eliminating furniture helps to balance the canoe, and it also gives children more foot space to successfully navigate the classroom. Too much furniture causes cramped and overcrowded conditions, which may cause behavior problems.

To effectively use the space in your classroom, you must understand how children use the square footage. Early childhood expert Frances Carlson suggests conducting a usage assessment by observing where and for how long children play in specific areas throughout the day. Keep track of the number of children and the amount of time each child spends in the various interest areas.

Although you might have a pretty good idea of where children spend their time and which centers are most popular, you may find that some areas are rarely frequented. If an area is underused, try adding interesting and new materials to enrich it and encourage children to visit. On the other hand, the usage assessment might reveal there are too many children vying for space, such as in the dramatic play or art areas, so it may be necessary to increase the size of some centers while decreasing space in others. By aligning children's usage with the center's size, it is possible to use all areas to their full capacity while maximizing available floor space.

Most importantly, design the classroom so the greatest amount of space is used for the largest amount of time with the greatest number of children. Once the classroom canoe is balanced, get ready to be amazed with many positive results for the children's happiness and behavior.

Reasons for Balancing the Classroom Canoe

- Less conflict and negative behavior

- Increased positive interactions with others

- More space for children's freedom of movement

- Improved usage of the entire classroom

- Reduced feeling of confinement

Balancing the Infant Classroom Canoe

Balancing the canoe in the infant room is a little more complicated. The first complication is the presence of cribs (both sleeping and evacuation). Because of mandated rules from the fire marshal and board of health inspectors, positioning cribs is always a conundrum. Typically, cribs end up around the room's perimeter—sometimes taking up as much as 30 percent of the room—leaving only the middle of the room for infant tummy and play time.

The second complication is the flooring. Many infant rooms have both carpet and tile installed in different sections of the rooms. The type of flooring dictates what types of activities are going to occur in the section, so how the area is going to be used has pretty much already been decided for you. For example, the carpet may be a good area for tummy time, while the tiled area might be a good area for diapering or eating. Too much carpet and not enough tile limits infants' activities and a balanced usage of the space. When there is too much tile and not enough carpeted spaces, the classroom space becomes unbalanced and so teachers use mats or area rugs to create sufficient space for babies to be on the floor.

Other areas of complexity are the changing table, feeding tables, and/or high and low chairs. They are usually located on tile and generally take up a large portion of the tiled section of the classroom, causing the area to be overloaded and leaving little foot space for either the caregivers or infants.

The final challenge is what author Jim Greenman calls "bunching up." This is a situation where the majority of adults and babies end up packing together and using only a limited amount of the available space. Perhaps this is the main reason for an unbalanced canoe: everyone (and even a good deal of toys and manipulatives) is located in one quadrant.

All of these complications invariably result in an imbalance—either in the space the furniture occupies or the usage of the furniture. For example, although the small eating table and chairs take up a good deal of square footage, they are rarely used more than for daily meals and possibly an occasional art experience. The same idea applies to the cribs. There is a lot of space devoted to cribs, yet the amount of time spent in the crib is significantly less than the amount of time that the babies spend on the floor.

▲ Before

The eight infants in this classroom spent the majority of the day bunched together on the blue mat behind the low shelving unit located in the middle of the room. The room was unbalanced because most available space was unused. The blue and green mats, which are taking up most of the carpeted area, were set up for two babies, one of whom was a crawler and one who was almost crawling. This climbing area was rarely used by the climbers. The eating area (obstructed by multicolored mats) located far right on tile was only used for eating. All the square footage in front of the toy shelves (in the middle of the room) was not being used.

▲ After

The room became more balanced when four destinations were created in different parts of the room for the children to occupy.

- One mat was moved behind the shelving unit.

- The sensory table was set up near the rocking chair.

- The blue mat and jungle-gym apparatus were placed together in the front right.

- The green and red climbing area were moved to the room's front left section.

For the majority of the day, the caregivers and infants visited each of the four areas in order to offer the babies a change of scenery and a variety of visual and physical experiences.

Types of Classroom Balance

In addition to the balance of furniture and its usage by children, there are other types of balance to consider: symmetrical, asymmetrical, and radial. As you go about designing the classroom space, pay attention to these three types of balance.

Symmetrical Balance

Symmetrical balance is achieved when objects are repeated, or mirrored, along a central axis. Symmetry can be found left to right (horizontally) and top to bottom (vertically). Symmetry achieves balance when things are the same on either side of the red line. In the photos to the right, the red line represents the central axis, so the symmetrical balance is horizontal. Symmetrical balance is easily created. For example, the teacher in this classroom achieved symmetry by balancing similar objects on either side of the imaginary red line. Notice the way that the bookshelves, lights, mailboxes, and children's work are repeated on both sides of the red line. Also note how the picture of the tree is centered in the middle of the design. Although the area is filled with objects and materials, the symmetrical balance helps children to process the information. The art shelf and dramatic play center are good examples of symmetrical balance.

Asymmetrical Balance

Asymmetrical balance is achieved through the balance of different elements on either side of the imaginary red line that have equal visual weight. Rather than repeating the same item on either side of the red line, asymmetrical balance uses different elements that possess a similar perceived weight on either side of the line. Using asymmetrical balance in a classroom gives a more dynamic feeling to the space. In the illustration on the top right, horizontal balance is maintained on either side of the red line, but the objects are not identical—only similar in weight. The star on the left side of the red line is equal in weight to the two triangles on the right.

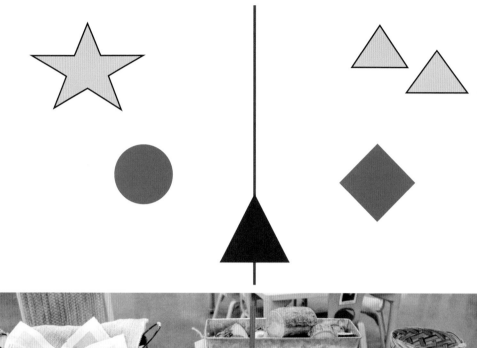

▲ This image is an example of asymmetrical balance because there are objects with similar visual weight on either side of the red line.

Radial Balance

Radial balance is based on the center of a circle, such as the circular table in the science corner or the group-meeting area's circular rug. The best way to understand radial balance is by thinking of a compass with the direction needle pointing out from the center. On all the outer circumference points of the compass, there is a balance of furniture.

In the illustration on the top right, the objects are balanced on the circle's circumference. Although there are different objects on the circumference, each object is of equal weight and they are equally distributed around the circle.

You can also achieve symmetry with a design rule known as the *rule of three*. With this rule, three objects are positioned on either side of an imaginary red line. The object positioned in the middle is a center interest point, or the focal point.

There is a general rule of thumb that says arranging with an odd number of objects is best for visual clarity. Three in a group seems to be the magic number, but five, seven, or nine objects in a grouping will also work.

Another design trick that can help create balance is the *triangle rule*. To use this rule, put the largest object as the center focal point (on the red line) and create balance on either side of the triangle with objects of similar visual weight.

Early childhood classrooms are busy and active places. Striking the right balance in a room can be a challenge, but applying principles of symmetry can help you transform your space into a balanced classroom canoe.

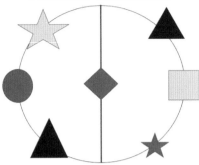

Radial Balance

Central Focus Point
Largest Object (size)

The Triangle Rule

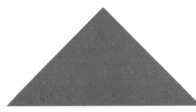

4

Classroom Design: Taking Cues
from Other Professions

The core of education is learning from others. We learn from family, parents, teachers, neighbors, friends, and relatives. The majority of our knowledge comes from what has been said, written, or shown to us. We also learn from our surroundings. An expert sailor navigating the high seas, for example, has learned the emerging whitecaps mean an increase in wind speed. From past experiences with the environment, the sailor has learned the importance of adjusting the boat's sails for the impending heavy winds. The fruit farmer carefully observes the orchard and surrounding conditions for pests, diseases, and possibly damaging weather conditions. Like the sailor and farmer, we can learn about ourselves and the world around us by taking cues from the environment and from others.

When designing classroom environments for young children, the early childhood practitioner also uses ideas learned from others. Such design ideas may include positioning quiet areas away from noisy areas, placing the painting easel near a water source, and keeping the block center away from high foot traffic. Regardless of who or where the ideas came from, this information is based on educational viewpoints and perspectives.

What would happen if educators started looking to other professional fields to gain ideas about classroom design? Perhaps we could learn from an interior decorator who uses room décor, such as mirrors or smaller furniture, to make a small room look larger. A textured mural hanging in a large hotel lobby makes the space feel cozier and more intimate. Smart designers manipulate the space and its furnishings because they want users to perceive something that makes them feel more comfortable. When they select furnishings and position them in a certain way, they are intentional about what, where, and why. Let's take some cues from experts in other fields about how we might design and furnish early childhood classrooms.

Furniture Designers: Lessons on Form and Shape

Design is a powerful tool. Furniture designers can teach us a great deal about form and shape because they understand how the psychology of design influences people's behaviors. Science has shown, for instance, that people react differently to design elements in furniture.

Round Shapes Elicit Calm

If you were in the market for new living room furniture for your home, would you be attracted to pieces with round and relaxed lines or furniture with sharp angular edges and straight lines? The research of Moshe Bar and Maital Neta, as well as that of Paul Silvia and Christopher Barona, shows how people react differently to round versus angular furniture and room layout. When both types of shapes (curved and angular) are balanced and symmetrical, the rounder shapes were preferred over angular. Silvia and Barona's fascinating research says that free-flowing curved forms are more compatible with the human mind. Curved or circular lines provide relief to the eyes and, according to these researchers, balance the harshness of straight, angular lines. Compared to rectilinear forms (sharp angles), curves and rounded edges foster a more pleasant and positive effect on people's emotions and sense of well-being. Participants in the research responded more positively to a furniture style and layout of curvilinear lines. When in the environment with soft, shallow curves, the participants felt increased pleasant emotions such as happiness, peacefulness, and relaxation.

Another interesting result of Silvia and Barona's research is that participants in the research were more likely to approach the curvilinear environment (and with more frequency) than they were to approach the rectilinear layout and square, angled furniture. Also, the participants in the curvilinear environment were more engaged, showing increased conversation, positive body language, and closer proximity with others, than those in the rectilinear environment. The research concluded that participants in the curvilinear environment felt more pleasant emotions, and their social interaction with others positively increased.

▲ Rectilinear environment

Seda Dazkir and Marilyn Read substantiated Silvia and Barona's research when they discovered that the shapes and forms of furniture have a significant effect on our emotions. The researchers simulated distinctively different interior settings: two settings held curvilinear (round) furniture, and two settings held rectilinear (angular) furniture. Dazkir and Read found that the settings with round furniture created significantly stronger positive and pleasant emotions with the study's participants. These positive emotions included relaxation, peace, and calm. The study's participants also approached the curvilinear settings and furniture forms with more frequency than they did the settings with angular furniture. The researchers concluded that furniture forms and furniture arrangements can have a distinct influence on our emotions and responses in interior environments.

What does this mean for the early childhood classroom? To design an environment that promotes children's well-being and social interaction, be sure to include curves in the classroom's furnishings and layout. Curves wider than 90 degrees, according to design expert Anita Rui Olds, invite us to "nest and inhabit a space; whereas, sharp angles seem cold and rejecting."

▲ Curvilinear environment

Table Shape and Size Matters

Look into almost any early childhood classroom and you will see an ocean of angular furniture and furnishings: cubbies, tables, windows, easels, bulletin boards, walls, and shelving units. One of the most prevalent sources of the angular shape in an early childhood classroom is the tables.

Shape: Circular tables increase children's well-being and engagement.

Size: Smaller tables promote children's socialization.

Table size and shape matters in the early childhood classroom.

The rectangle is the most commonly found table shape in the classroom and is especially favored for mealtimes. Perhaps rectangular tables are popular because many children can comfortably sit around them. Or, maybe they are favored because most classrooms are small and rectangular shapes fit better into the available space. Regardless, tables are an important—but sometimes overlooked—classroom element influencing children's well-being and social development.

Take a mental inventory of the tables in your classroom. Are there more rectangular than circular tables? Are there more large tables than small? Probably so. Because it is impractical and financially infeasible, however, to change out perfectly good rectangular tables for circular tables, consider infusing curves and soft, rounded shapes into the classroom in other ways.

Curves can be infused into the early childhood classroom with other types of furnishings such as stools, chairs, shelving units, and rugs. Think about the following suggestions for your classroom.

- Find a small stool to place in the library corner. Not only does a small stool add soft curves to the classroom, it doesn't take up much room and certainly offers a special place to sit.

- Adding a circular ottoman is another idea. You can usually find one at home-goods stores, and they are relatively inexpensive, especially if you look for faux leather, which is easy to clean and very durable.

- Add curves to the classroom with oval or round rugs. Use small round rugs under the home living table or to anchor a piece of furniture in the middle of the room. Half-circle rugs are also an option for infusing curvilinear shapes into the environment. Because half-circle rugs are typically smaller in size, they work great in front of small shelving units, under a small rocking chair, or in front of the kitchen sink in the home living area.

- Look for circular pillows rather than the typical square or rectangle shape to add to the classroom.

▲ Two circular elements (table and stool) made this a charming place for clay play. Note the table's drawer for extra storage.

▲ Many ottomans are circular and can be found at home-good or resale stores. Some ottomans have the extra advantage of storage.

Wallpaper Designers: Lessons about Lines

Wallpaper designers are experts in understanding the importance of lines. Lines affect how space is perceived: They can lead your eyes upward or they can express movement and direction. Lines can give a room energy, whether calming or chaotic. A line can be combined with another line or many lines, resulting in simple or complex patterns. Squiggly lines can convey a sense of chaos or loss of control. Wavy lines can communicate freedom or continuity, such as waves crashing on the shore. Lines tightly drawn and close together suggest confinement. The most important property of a line is its direction, be it horizontal, vertical, curving, or diagonal, because the line's directionality leads the eye and creates visual focus. When designing a classroom, be intentional about horizontal and vertical lines, whether they are inherently in the space or placed there.

Horizontal Lines

Horizontal lines communicate a sense of peace and quiet, rest and stability. They can symbolize tranquility. Horizontal lines give a relaxed informal feeling, and because these types of lines suggest width, horizontal lines can visually expand a space.

Designing a classroom with horizontal lines all at the same height creates an expansive and open feeling. Horizontal lines lead the eye, and eyes can send messages to the body, so these types of lines give a sense of freedom to move about the space unencumbered. If you do not have the luxury of having cabinets all the same height, combine cabinets of the same height together in a specific space or learning center. In this classroom, for example, most of the shelves are the same height in certain areas, which creates a consistent horizontal line within each center.

Vertical Lines

Vertical lines suggest reaching upward. These types of lines represent strength, power, and stability. Vertical lines seem to hold the force of gravity like a stake in the ground, so they generate feelings of steadiness. Most importantly, vertical lines extend away from our visual plane so they create a sense of height in a space. When the ceiling feels like it is pushing down, add vertical lines to create a sense of height.

In this image, note how the canopy over the housekeeping center moves your eye up and adds an expansive feeling to this space. Although there are many horizontal lines from the shelves and tables in the space, the vertical lines of the canopy create visual balance and add a sense of height in this small classroom. Additionally, the canopy adds a focal point to the home living area.

What does this mean for early childhood classrooms? Lines are indeed powerful and can tell a visual story. Vertical lines are awake, alert, rigid, strong, and stable; whereas, horizontal lines are restful and serene. Combine a horizontal line with a vertical line, and the result is stillness and equilibrium. Consider the following design tips on how to use lines to their best advantage in the classroom.

- Use vertical lines to create a sense of height in the space.

- Place flat horizontal surfaces of equal height near each other to help expand the space and create harmony. Remember that horizontal lines bring the eyes down.

- Use vertical lines that are connected at the top to make a space look cozier and more confined.

- Use horizontal lines connected at the bottom to lift up the space and make it look lighter and happier.

- Use a vertical line that connects with a horizontal line to make the space feel more balanced and still.

▲ Colors that reflect nature, such as blues and greens, are a calming influence in the classroom.

Interior Decorators: Lessons on Color

Interior decorators play with color schemes. They understand how to use color to great advantage and recognize the effect color has on mood and behavior. It has been said that when the color is right, the mood is right. Experts in the psychology of color, such as Texas Tech University's Kristi Gaines and Zane Curry, assert that color is a powerful element of classroom design because children's responses to color are both emotional and physiological. The psychological effect of color produces profound changes in emotional comfort and mood, while the physiological effect influences children's levels of engagement and attention.

Physiological Effects

Kathie Engelbrecht's research on the physiological effect of color illustrated that when a person experiences different colors, certain hormones are released into the brain. These hormones significantly affect an individual's energy levels, moods, and mental acuity. The color red, for example, has a tendency to overstimulate as well as cause an increase in heart rate and blood pressure and to heighten the sense of smell. Concurring research by Harry Wolfarth and Catherine Sam found that color changes in the environment, especially changes from bright colors to more subdued and subtle colors, result in decreased pulse rates and lowered body temperatures. Further, researcher Preeti Verghese contends that classroom designers should consider the quantity of color used in indoor spaces. This is especially true when using primary colors— red, yellow, and blue—and colors with high intensity, such as bright orange and neon purple. Because the human mind is wired to make connections, find patterns, and organize visual information, too much color and too many colors in young children's environments distracts their brains from doing its job.

▲ Pink is known for having a calming influence on people's moods and behaviors, which is perfect for naptime.

Psychological Effects

The psychology of color and its psychological effects on people is a much-researched subject. Research has shown that color can change people's moods, energy levels, and focus. Researcher Alexander Schauss was the first to report how prisoners' moods calmed and their angry behaviors lessened when wearing pink prisoner garb. In his book *The Power of Color*, color psychologist, Morton Walker agrees with Schauss and cites several examples of the influence of color on people's moods and behaviors: Weightlifters have more powerful performances in gyms painted blue. Babies cry more frequently in yellow rooms. Juvenile delinquents exhibit less negative behavior when put in holding tanks that are painted pink.

Scientific studies have proven that children with attention-deficit disorders or sensory integration issues are extremely affected by the colors in a learning environment. Kristi Gaines and Zane Curry's research determined that this reaction happens because color speaks to our emotional as well as our physical selves.

Colors are divided into two groups: warm and cool. According to the research review by Soma Kalia on color and its effects in interior environments, one group of colors is not better than the other. Rather, these two groups have different emotional effects on a space. Reds, yellows, and oranges are warm colors, which stimulate and excite. Blues, greens, and purples are cool colors, which have a relaxing and calming influence on the environment.

Color is the first element we register when we look at objects. Each color has a specific wavelength that affects the senses. Viewing calming colors, for example, lowers the heart rate, while seeing stimulating colors results in an increasing heart rate. Children with sensory integration issues are more comfortable with cool colors. Author of *In My World: Designing Living and Learning Environments for the Young* Ro Logrippo believes that active children are more comfortable with cool colors and that passive children prefer warm colors. Additionally, it appears that children have distinct color preferences. Research conducted by Chris Boyatzis and Reenu Varghese investigated children's emotional associations with colors. The researchers questioned thirty girls and thirty boys, ages five years to six-and-a-half years old. The children were shown nine different colors, one at a time, and asked "How does this color make you feel?" Regardless of their age, the study's participants were able to verbally express their preferences and connect certain colors to either positive or negative emotions. Overall, children voiced negative emotions when presented darker—black and brown—colors; they expressed positive reactions to bright colors such as pink and blue. In other words, the children had a preference of colors and their preferences were significantly linked to either positive or negative emotions.

What does this mean for early childhood classrooms? Color plays a big role in making a classroom more attractive, but it also plays other roles, such as absorbing or reflecting light, changing the perception of how big or small a room is, and affecting the mood of those who abide within the space. Early childhood expert Sony Vasandani asserts that color can elicit positive or negative feelings that, in turn, affect children's behaviors, moods, and ultimately their learning. Consider the following ideas when it's time to paint the classroom's walls.

- Bright colors tend to be overstimulating.

- Darker colors can make a small room look even smaller.

- Neutral colors on furniture help to convey a natural and calming ambiance.

- Pure white reflects light and can be hard on the eyes.

- Blue-green and violet hues are relaxing and comforting colors.

- Mellow yellows are perceived as cheerful colors and are known to stimulate brain activity.

- Red increases heart rate, excitement, and activity level.

- Bright oranges can be perceived as distressing and upsetting.

What to do with primary-colored furniture? Many classrooms are equipped with such furniture. Although neutral colors help to convey a more natural and calming ambiance, most of us cannot afford to purchase all new oak or light-colored furniture. What can you do to make the classroom appear more neutral? Try these suggestions.

- If you have different colored chairs in the room, place like-colored chairs together. For example, place all red chairs under one table and all yellow chairs under another table.

- If you have a multicolored rug, try flipping it over. Is the backside of the rug a neutral color, and would it be comfortable enough to use in the home living area?

- Keep like-colored shelving units together in a learning center. So, you might place the green shelves in the science corner, while you place the yellow shelves in the dramatic play area.

- Introduce greenery into the classroom, which has a tendency to soften primary colors.

- If the table in the home living area is a primary color, use a neutral-colored tablecloth to hide the tabletop. For primary-colored chairs, place neutral-colored slipcovers over the backs. Sometimes pillowcases will work for this purpose.

- If you have primary-colored pillows in the classroom, sew new cases made from neutral colors (or find someone who can do it for you). Don't have access to a sewing machine? Look for neutral-colored pillow shams on sale at a home-goods store. Pillow shams are an especially good option because when they get dirty you can simply throw them in the washing machine to clean.

Horticulturalists: Lessons about Nature

A horticulturist is a person who uses scientific knowledge to cultivate plants and flowers. The primary job of a horticulturist is to propagate and generate more plants, especially those of higher quality and beauty. Horticulturists do much of their work in a greenhouse. Teachers of young children can take cues from horticulturists by creating a greenhouse classroom filled with natural elements.

Richard Louv, author of *Last Child in the Woods*, links the absence, or deficit, of nature in our lives to some disturbing trends in young children: the rise in obesity, depression, and attention disorders. He coined the term *nature-deficit disorder* to explain the phenomenon of children experiencing little connection with nature and the natural world, and he believes childhood is in jeopardy because of this syndrome. The American Psychological Association identifies nature-deficit disorders, which include stress and attention-deficit disorders, as a top mental health concern for young children. The research of McCurdy, Winterbottom, Mehta, and Roberts confirmed that the sedentary indoor lifestyle of many children is a major contributing factor in the increase of chronic health maladies such as diabetes, asthma, hypertension, and vitamin D deficiencies.

Caution: Whatever plants you choose, make sure they are nontoxic.

▲ Without greenery

▼ With greenery

Research conducted separately by Roger Ulrich and Virginia Lohr found that people who work in environments filled with live plants and green foliage were more productive than those working in environments without interior plants. Just being able to see greenery helps to reduce blood pressure and lessen stress. A 1984 hospital study by Roger Ulrich found that surgical patients who had views of trees had less need for pain medication and healed faster than those with views of a brick wall. There was also a substantial difference in the stress levels experienced by the patients with a tree view. The benefits of live plants are not limited to adults. In a study involving children with attention deficits, for example, Andrea Fabor Taylor and Francis Kuo discovered that children exhibit higher levels of concentration after a walk in the park.

The solution to nature-deficit disorder is relatively simple and twofold: Take children outside, and bring nature inside. In her book *The Great Outdoors*, nature advocate Mary Rivkin encourages outdoor play as a simple matter of being human: "We are nature. We have not evolved beyond nature, we are still inextricably linked . . . To be fully human, we need to connect with nature." In his book *Natural Playscapes: Creating Outdoor Play Environments for the Soul*, Rusty Keeler urges teachers to take children outside, to create natural play environments, and to let children play. His vision of a perfect place for children to play is not your everyday, run-of-the-mill playground with its typical fixed equipment, metal or PVC play pieces, and safety fall zones. Rather, Keeler advocates what he calls *playscapes*, which are filled with natural elements for the children to experience through all of their senses. Natural playscapes are outdoor spaces that encourage children to experience the world with their whole being. Playscapes speak to children's spirits as they encounter nature in all its beauty, joy, and wonder. Nature advocate and executive director of Nature Explore, Nancy Rosenow, has identified a variety of natural experiences that positively affect the children's quality of life in the outdoors, such as climbing trees, building forts and lean-to structures, growing gardens, wading in creeks, and rolling in crispy autumn leaves.

In addition to getting outside, bringing nature inside is another effective way to reduce nature-deficit disorder in young children. To get started, follow the advice that authors Sandra Duncan and Jody Martin suggest in their book *Bringing the Outside In.*

- Look for nature in unexpected places, and you will quickly discover nature all around: in parking lots, alleyways, parks, sidewalks, and neighborhood yards.

- Use natural elements to create art. Children will delight in the beauty of nature's textures, colors, and patterns and in making magnificent nature the subject of their art.

- Infuse nature in every nook and cranny in the classroom. Think beyond the science corner, and include nature or natural elements in all areas and on all surfaces. Place gourds or pumpkins on the table in the home living center, or include twigs for writing tools or paintbrushes in the art area. Use seashells or pebbles for counting in the mathematics center. Put seashells with holes for stringing in the manipulative area.

- Include living things in the classroom, such as sweet potato vines or herbs, an aquarium, container gardens, hermit crabs, roly-poly bugs, or pond jars.

What does this mean for early childhood classrooms? Early childhood classrooms are often devoid of nature and natural elements. Although we are particular about putting the right number and type of books in the classroom and making sure there are enough blocks, puzzles, and art supplies, we often overlook adding nature and natural elements into the environment. These elements can improve children's focus and concentration—especially for younger children or children with attention-deficit disorders. The benefits of bringing nature into the classroom are well-documented in research studies. Nature activists Robin Moore and Allen Cooper, with the Natural Learning Initiative at North Carolina State University, assert that children who have frequent exposure and interaction with nature experience enhanced cognition, increased positive behaviors, improved academic performance, better problem-solving skills, increased creativity, and greater attention and focus. Additionally, studies link nature-based learning with reduced attention-deficit disorder symptoms. Researcher Dana L. Miller asserts, for example, that children who experience frequent interactions and experiences with nature have increased focus, improved observational skills, and greater self-confidence. Nature-based learning, however, isn't something that only happens outdoors. Rather, learning through nature should occur both outside and inside the classroom. Consider the following ideas.

- **Cherish the window view.** If you are lucky enough to have a window to the outside, do not block the natural light with opaque materials such as construction paper. Use the natural light coming into the space as a learning tool. Place prisms, reflective objects, and translucent items to capture the reflections and shadows of the sunlight.

- **Set up an aquarium filled with colorful fish.** Add a fishbowl or aquaponics fish bowl with a Beta fish to your classroom. Position the fishbowl or aquarium at the children's eye level so they can see the fish swimming and eating. For older children, try placing the fishbowl in the art center, quiet area, or lunch table to encourage inspiration and conversation.

- **Infuse the classroom with at least four different types of live plants with green foliage.** Choose a variety of plants to offer different textures, scents, and sizes. Consider Boston fern, African violet, rosemary, and cacti. Whichever plants you choose, be sure they are nontoxic.

- **Include nature in every area of the classroom.** Use rocks for counting or game pieces in the math area. Pinecones in the home living area can represent noodles in the pretend chicken soup, along with a piece of driftwood to use as a soup spoon. Different sizes and shapes of seashells in the science corner are fun to weigh and compare. Include birch bark or large leaves in the art center for uniquely different papers for painting. Note: Do not pull bark off a live tree. This could seriously damage the tree.

- **Record nature sounds and play them during naptime or while children are playing.** You may also wish to use the following websites for prerecorded nature sounds:
  www.naturesongs.com, www.naturesound.org, www.listeningearth.com,
  www.soundcloud.com, www.youtube.com/watch?v=b2njHW9ydWs, or
  www.makeuseof.com/tag/discover-sound-nature-youtube

- **Project videos of nature in the classroom.** Load videos of birds, animals, ocean waves, streams, and butterflies on a portable pocket HDMI travel projector. Simply connect the projector to your phone and project a video on an open wall.

- **Take photographs of nature around the neighborhood.** Look for different types of trees, flowers, a farmers' market, water, and the sky. Find a company that can enlarge the photos and affix them to canvasses, and then hang them around the classroom. Another idea is to have children take the pictures. You are sure to get a new perspective! If photography isn't your forte, look for framed landscapes in a secondhand store.

- **Infuse natural elements.** Search for wicker baskets and wood or bamboo placemats to add to the classroom. Burlap and cork are also good choices. Find some wildflowers and display them in a vase (or many vases for that matter), and then place the vase in the middle of the lunch or home living table. Beautiful brown cattails can be found near areas with water. Once cut, place in a vase without water; they will keep forever. Spraying the cattails with clear acrylic (when children are not around) helps prolong their display life. Planter boxes filled with sun-loving plants add greenery to the classroom. If you don't have a planter box, there are lots of inexpensive or even free containers you could use, including buckets, tin boxes and cans, children's shoes and boots, or liter soda bottles with their tops cut off.

▼ Tin cans make wonderful indoor mini-gardens.

- **Encourage children to string seashells on twine or fishing line, and then hang it in a sunlit area.** If you have a chance to visit a beach, look for seashells with holes in them. Work with children to build a mobile from seashells, twine, and small sticks. It's a great exercise in problem solving, critical thinking, and creativity. Find a special place to hang the mobile. Not only will it add beauty to the classroom, but children will also have a sense of ownership since they created it. If you teach in a classroom with children in diapers, hang the mobile above the changing table. Be sure it is low enough so the child's view looking up is interesting. Gently nudging the shells creates a visual and auditory interest for the little ones.

Live Plants and Flowers

Live plants and flowers add an ambiance of beauty to the early childhood classroom. Live greenery not only brightens a space, but it can also improve air quality. Adding plants to interior spaces increases oxygen levels. A number of research studies with both students and workers revealed that the presence of plants can have a huge effect on air quality and well-being. Researcher B. C. Wolverton discovered that when spider plants are contained in a sealed chamber, they remove 95 percent of formaldehyde from the air during a period of twenty-four hours. Formaldehyde fumes, which irritate mucous membranes, come from particle board, varnishes, and—most disconcerting because many classrooms have them—ceiling tiles. The research illustrated how such toxins are absorbed through plants' leaves and neutralized in the soil. A University of Michigan study that found plants in the environment improved concentration, memory, and productivity. Being "under the influence of plants" can increase adults' memory retention up to 20 percent. Just think what plants in the classroom can do for young children!

Consider adding plants such as snake plant, African violet, bird's nest fern, begonia, prayer plant, Warneck dracaena, spider plant, bamboo palm, Chinese evergreen, Boston fern, and cacti or other succulents. Some teachers shy away from cacti because of their prickly needles, but they are really quite harmless if you choose plants without the minutely thin needles. Look for succulents such as *Echeveria peacockii*, one of the genus *Argyroderma* (also called ice plant), or *Sedum nussbaumerianum* (also called coppertone stonecrop), which are not prickly.

Spider plants are a particularly interesting plant to have in the classroom because they grow at a rapid rate, and children are fascinated with the plant's baby plantlets. Cut away the plantlet from the main part of the plant, press it into soil, add water, and pretty soon there will be another spider plant growing! For a list of nontoxic plants, visit https://dengarden.com/gardening/Non-Toxic-House-Plants-For-Homes-Children-Cats-and-Dogs

Classroom plants provide advantages beyond improving air quality. Children benefit from learning how to care for and nurture a living thing, which encourages self-confidence and a sense of responsibility. When children are vested in the care of classroom plants, they notice the many changes such as a new sprout, leaf, or blossom. These observations bring a keen awareness of the world around them. For many children, this awareness leads to feelings of responsibility and commitment to caring for the earth.

Dried Flowers and Plants

During the summer, colorful outdoor flowers and plants are plentiful. Save their beauty by drying the flowers and then displaying them in the winter. Although there are several methods of drying (or pressing) flowers, the easiest method is to put the flowers in the pages of a magazine or book. Place one or two flowers in the pages of a thick hardcover book, then cover the book with a heavy object, such as a pan or brick. Leave the flowers in the book for at least two weeks, though more time may be needed. You may wish to display the dried flowers by placing them in a vase where everyone can enjoy their beauty. Because dried flowers are extremely fragile, find a place for them where they won't be accidentally bumped. Another idea is to press the flowers between laminated sheets to make book markers, a picture to frame, or an ornament to hangRead more about preserving and drying plants at Gardening Know How: https://www.gardeningknowhow.com/garden-how-to/projects/drying-flowers-and-foliage.htm

Even artificial flowers can add beauty and calm to the classroom space. A great source for inexpensive artificial flower arrangements is resale shops or rummage sales. Look for arrangements with green foliage, as green is the most natural color.

Nature Artifacts

Many interesting nature-made artifacts are ideal for the classroom, including the following:

- Turtle shell
- Snail shell
- Starfish
- Snake skin
- Petrified wood
- Geode
- River rock
- Bird feathers
- Shark teeth
- Seed pods
- Antlers
- Bark

▼ Natural artifacts such as seashells, a turtle shell, starfish, and an antler captivate young children and capture their attention and interest.

Trading Post

Children find nature-made artifacts fascinating; they love to closely examine these interesting objects by seeing, touching, and sometimes listening to them. You may want to add a nature artifact trading post to the classroom. Encourage children to bring small nature items to school, and then let them trade their precious found objects for another child's treasures, if they wish.

The size of the trading post will determine how large or small the artifacts can be, so it is important to discuss and determine size parameters of objects prior to opening the trading post. Encourage children to trade the natural objects in a fair way. If one object was brought to the trading post, only one object should be removed from the trading post. It's a great exercise in mathematics, responsibility, and self-regulation by learning about fairness and trust.

Workplace Productivity Experts: Lessons in Engagement

The need to ensure workplace productivity is as important to an employer as creating an appropriate classroom environment is to an early childhood educator. Why? We want people both old and young to be happy and to thrive in the environments designed for them. Early childhood teachers can learn how to design successful classrooms from other companies and organizations.

Google

This company takes pride in fostering a culture of creativity in the workplace. The freedom of creativity results in happy, motivated, and productive employees. Google works hard to provide a welcoming work environment and is famous for perks such as an onsite restaurant, game tables, gyms, and bowling alleys. Offices at Google do not resemble a typical corporate setting. Instead, the environment has been specifically and intentionally designed to encourage interaction and to support sharing ideas; it features flexible and easily movable furniture, soft seating, comfortable places for small groups to convene and brainstorm, glass walls in many work suites, and views of—as well as easy transitions to—the outside world.

▲ Young children have greater engagement and are more likely to follow classroom rules when they have been instrumental in creating them.

Community Health Center

In a study from Taiwan, researchers surveyed 1,380 staff members from 230 community health centers. Blossom Yen-Ju Lin and associates found that the ability to make decisions independently was highly linked to job satisfaction. The study found that the more autonomy employees have at work, the more satisfied they are and the less likely they are to leave their jobs.

Virgin Management

Virgin Management asked its employees for their ideas about what they would like to see in a workplace environment. Their responses addressed what they wanted the workplace to look like aesthetically as well as some improvements that would make their spaces more environmentally friendly. When people are involved in the decision making or actually creating the surroundings, they are empowered to be engaged, productive, and, therefore, happier.

What does this mean for early childhood classrooms? Prakash Nair, Randall Fielding, and Jeffrey Lackney's book, *The Language of School Design: Design Patterns for 21st Century Schools*, encourages including children in design choices. Think about how many times you have invited children to help in the design of the classroom. It's simply not often a consideration, which is understandable. For the most part, children have very little input into the environments they use, but there are ways to involve young children in classroom design. Try some of the following ideas to engage your young learners.

- When you are considering a change in the classroom, open the discussion at group time and listen to children's ideas.

- Ask children for suggestions about what materials they would like to see added to a specific area, such as a writing or science area.

- Invite children to help make classroom rules, and then encourage them to create a poster or sign announcing these rules.

- Offer a section of the room that is not devoted to anything and is devoid of all equipment, furnishings, and materials. Let the children decide what should be in this vacant space.

Offer children opportunities to give tours to classmates and teachers. Encourage children to explain the different areas in the classroom and also to give their ideas on ways to improve the spaces. Child-led tours may be conducted by an individual child, in pairs, or even small groups. Elect a student photographer to document the tour. During the child-led tours, take notes and snap pictures with your camera or smartphone. Ask questions and encourage children's conversations. After the child-led tour, meet with the children and listen to their ideas and suggestions. You may want to record and post their ideas.

If children's ideas are feasible, create a plan of action with them, and implement suggestions for improvement as soon as possible. If children's suggested ideas are unrealistic, try to offer alternatives that will help them understand the concept of exploring options and compromise when working together for a common goal. If children's ideas are too grandiose, suggest a smaller version of the idea. According to early childhood expert and author Michelle Salcedo, a rotating center based on children's interests and needs is a good addition to the classroom. Give children the opportunity to decide what the area will be and the materials to include. When children's interests change or they grow weary of what is in the space, ask them to suggest new ideas.

Just as it is important for workplace productivity experts to understand the psychology of employee satisfaction and how to promote worker productivity, it is important for early childhood practitioners to understand children's happiness and interest in the classroom surroundings. Children, like adults in the workplace, spend a large part of their day in the classroom. Encouraging children to contribute to the classroom design promotes self-awareness and self-confidence, which is better known in education as academic, social, and emotional success.

Grocery Store Manager: Lessons about Display

The job of a grocery store retailer is encouraging shoppers to spend money on groceries. Grocery store retailers understand the psychology behind consumer purchasing and use this knowledge when designing the store's layout and determining product placement. Experts in consumer behavior, grocery managers design the spaces so shoppers will spend as much time as possible in the store. The more time spent, the more money is usually spent. Grocers are also well aware of shoppers' buying habits and know how to attract their attention. In addition to the store's well-crafted layout, shelves are stocked in a specific way to attract buyers to their contents and, ultimately, to influence their decision to spend more money. Grocers use many design strategies such as dual placement, shelf stocking, visual purchasing, the science of planograms, and optimizing dwell time. Early childhood teachers can learn from grocers about effective ways to design and manage the shelves in the classroom to increase children's engagement.

Dual Placement

Dual placement means that the grocer places an identical product in several different locations so shoppers can find the same item in more than one section of the store. A specific salsa brand, for example, might be found in many sections: chips and crackers, ethnic food, the salsa section, and even in cold foods. Because shoppers possibly see this product several times in the store, they may be more likely to notice it, pick it up, and put it in their baskets.

End caps are frequently used for dual product placement. The end caps are the shelves located on both ends of an aisle. Because they provide increased visibility for a product, they are premium spots in the store. In addition to dual placement, they are often used to introduce a new product, promote products on sale, or inspire the use of a product. The customer sees items placed on the end cap, thinks they are needed, and throws them into the grocery cart. Vendors pay extra for their product to be located on an end cap, which gives them increased visibility, which translates to increased sales.

Use the grocer's cross-merchandising idea as an effective design strategy for the early childhood classroom. Just as the grocer strategically places the salsa in many different areas of the store, you can position identical materials in different areas of the classroom for maximum use. For example, place storybooks in the quiet or library area, and also place them in each learning area of the classroom. Recipe books donated by families or purchased at the local resale shop are terrific additions to the home living or kitchen area. Books about constructing and building are perfect for the block center. National Geographic and DK books have gorgeous photographs of people, animals, and land, so they make nice additions to the science area. Placing books in many different areas of the classroom will give children ample opportunities to explore the materials.

Use the grocer's ideas about end caps by setting up a table in a walk-by area. After an interesting field trip, for example, display artifacts such as photographs, programs, pamphlets, and souvenirs. Include storybooks and images reflecting the place visited. Invite children to share their artwork, sketches, and writings about the trip on the table.

▲ Ensure shelves are organized, with materials readily visible and displayed in aesthetically pleasing ways.

Shelf-Stocking

The way shelves are stocked with groceries has a significant effect on customer purchasing. In most instances, there are three layers of shelves in a grocery store: bottom, middle, and top. The bottom shelf typically holds less expensive generic and store brands and may include bulk foods. The top shelf holds items that don't sell quickly, such as specialty, gourmet, and locally sourced products. The middle shelf is at the consumer's eye level and, therefore, is considered the bull's-eye zone and a favored place for vendors to display their goods. The middle shelf holds high-selling and well-known, leading brands sold at equally premium prices.

Use the grocer's shelf-stocking strategy in the design of your classroom shelves. Put the most interesting learning materials on the shelf with the most visibility to children. Do away with the items that have been on the shelves forever or the ordinary materials that have been purchased from a catalog. Instead, use the middle shelf for wow-worthy learning materials that are irresistible and will promote imagination and fascination.

Visual Purchasing

It has been said that people eat with their eyes first, which means that the food must look good as well as taste good. Grocers understand the importance of visually appealing displays, especially in the produce section, so they go to great lengths to display fruits and vegetables in aesthetically pleasing ways.

Help children have a better experience in perusing your classroom shelves by ensuring that the shelf displays are organized and the materials and supplies are readily visible. Materials and supplies need to be easy for children to select from the shelf and equally easy to return. Successful grocery stores are also well-stocked. This doesn't mean overstuffing and overloading the shelves, which can look messy and overwhelming. It does mean having stock nearby, in the back of the store, or in the warehouse. When a product runs short, the grocer simply replaces and replenishes.

The same is true for classroom shelves. Be mindful of the amount of materials placed on the shelves. There should be sufficient space between the containers so children can easily retrieve and replace the materials. Keep surplus materials in the teacher cabinet, and rotate materials when children's interests change.

Ineffective shelves are:

- overloaded with too many materials.

- cramped with materials placed too close together.

- stagnant, and the offerings seldom change.

- disorganized, and materials are hard to find.

- full of mixed materials from different subject areas.

Effective shelves are:

- stocked with materials that are rotated weekly.

- organized by type, with like materials together on the same shelf.

- consistent in their offerings, but also stocked with weekly surprises or mystery materials.

- arranged to give breathing room between materials for easy differentiation and selection.

- organized by subject area, with different topics located in different shelving units.

The Science of a Planogram

Visual purchasing isn't limited to the produce section but continues throughout the entire store. Imagine for a moment that chocolate is on a customer's grocery list. The customer goes to the aisle where chocolate is located and begins looking. There are lots of options: bag of chocolate or bar? dark chocolate or milk? raspberry filling or caramel? Grocers are aware that having lots of choices can be overwhelming, so they use a *planogram*, which is a visual representation of the consumer decision tree, to guide the customer's decision. Bags of chocolate are separated from chocolate bars. Different flavors of chocolate are designated by the bag's color and are easily recognizable. Similar bag colors, such as yellow bags of semi-sweet chocolate and gold bags of milk chocolate, are not placed together because the yellow color is too similar to the gold. Instead, the yellow and gold bags are separated by a red bag of chocolates. The desired product is easily distinguished from all the other chocolate on the shelf. Grocers and manufacturers understand that consumers do not spend a lot of time selecting products—mere seconds at best—so visibility and easy access to the desired product are extremely important to increasing the store's revenues.

The same is true for designing classroom shelves. To promote active engagement with classroom materials, you want customers (the children) to be visually attracted to the contents of your shelves. Attracting customers means that the shelves should be organized in a way that children can easily select their purchases (classroom materials) and return them to the shelf when ready. Take a cue from the grocer and use the planogram concept for effective shelving in the classroom.

Dwell Time

Consumer expert Paco Underhill, author of *Why We Buy: The Science of Shopping*, asserts that consumers have no intention of purchasing two-thirds of everything they buy in a grocery store. Grocery stores not only want this shopper behavior, but they also encourage it through the store's design and layout. One of the biggest strategies for encouraging impulsive buying is called *dwell time*. Although people make purchasing decisions in seconds, they often have to wait to check out at the cash register. During this dwell time in the check-out line, there is ample opportunity to find a magazine with a good article that you want to read, notice a candy bar that looks irresistible, or see a small gadget that you just cannot live without.

Use the grocer's strategy of dwell time if you have an unpopular or infrequently visited area in your classroom. Create a reason for children to come and dwell in the area. For example, in the science area, add seasonal objects such as a display of beautiful fall leaves along with magnifying glasses for viewing the leaves' veins and colors. Provide some tempera paint for children to use to paint and decorate the fall leaves. Or, place brown, crunchy leaves with a pestle and mortar so the children can pulverize the leaves. What child doesn't like to spend time pounding?

Considering Children's Needs

Since very early times, humans have needed to cultivate their surroundings to ensure survival. As humans, we seek environments with certain qualities that allow us to feel comfortable, and safety and security are typically high on the list. Other factors include temperature, light, fresh air, and positive stimuli.

Abraham Maslow, the acknowledged founder of humanistic psychology, believed that people are guided by a set of hierarchical needs. There are two types of basic needs, *physiological* and *psychological*. Physiological needs relate to the body, and psychological needs relate to feelings and emotional well-being. Maslow also postulated a higher-level needs category he called *self-actualization*, which includes the desire to feel fulfilled, gain skills and progress, and pursue talents and hobbies.

Maslow's Theory of Human Needs

- **Physiological needs:** related to bodily needs, such as food, shelter, warmth, and water

- **Psychological needs:** related to emotional needs, such as safety, belonging, love, and esteem

- **Higher-level needs:** related to self-actualization, such as growth, fulfillment, pursuing talents, and gaining skills

Early childhood practitioners can use these hierarchies to help design classroom spaces that address basic needs while also creating opportunities to fulfill higher-level needs. A well-rounded environment addresses and supports these needs.

Physiological Needs

Basic physiological needs include physical elements that are vital to the child's survival, such as food, shelter, warmth, water, oxygen, sleep, and clothing. If these needs are not met by the classroom environment and responsible caregivers, opportunities for growth will suffer. Imagine trying to listen to a teacher's instructions or to follow a story being read during story time when you are thirsty or cold. Would you not be distracted, perhaps even forgetting to listen to the story altogether because you are uncomfortable?

There is a significant link between classroom design and physiological needs: If the design and elements in the classroom do not satisfy children's physiological needs, then children's learning, growth, and development is in jeopardy. It is important, therefore, to be sure these needs are being met. Being cold, for example, distracts children from the tasks at hand, so be sure the classroom is devoid of drafts. Stick a small rug or towel at the gap in the bottom of a door that is letting in cold air. Place a blanket at the base of windows that are not properly sealed. Provide pillows, cushions, or a rug so children are not sitting on a cold tile floor. Ensure proper lighting by adding ambient lighting, such as table or floor lamps, or positioning the children near natural light or a source of electric light for story time, so they are able to see the storybooks from any angle.

▲ Children need environments that feel relaxed and full of ease.

Need for Safety

Children need to feel safe. They need to be in a space that allows their brains to rest from our overstimulated world. Like all living creatures that burrow into holes or build nests, our basic human instinct craves places to feel safe and protected. Finding smaller areas in the classroom that are comfortable and cozy is rather hard with institutional furniture, so try to have at least one piece of authentic furniture, such as a rocking chair, or provide extra-soft pillows (dog beds are soft, fairly inexpensive, and washable). Spaces where children can be alone ensure a consistent and reliable environment that helps them feel safe.

Offering thoughtfully designed areas for quiet and alone time can provide a sense of well-being, security, and comfort. The inclusion of elements such as pillows, cushions, baskets, and other natural items helps to ensure the classroom environment is a welcoming and nurturing space for young children to grow.

Need for Belonging and Love

Many children spend a great amount of time in the care of others, especially in child care centers. According to *Child Health USA 2014*, 12.5 million or 61.3 percent of preschool-aged children are in some form of child care for at least one day each week on a regular basis. Of those, 23.5 percent receive care in a center-based setting. Consequently, the classroom environment plays a significant nurturing role in their lives. To promote a sense of belonging, children need to feel connected to others and believe they can make important contributions to the group. Above all, children need to feel loved and celebrated.

Self-Esteem and Self-Actualization

Children need to believe they are an important force in the world. To promote and further this belief, early childhood classrooms must be designed so children have plenty of opportunities to demonstrate their competencies, practice their skills in leadership, and engage in collaboration and cooperation. The most important factor influencing children's belief of importance is freedom of choice. The freedom to choose means children are allowed to express and act on their preferences about materials and activities throughout their day.

Children who have opportunities to make choices, regardless of whether they make bad or good choices, early in life make better choices later in life. Children who are given opportunities to experience choice feel good and accomplished about their decisions, which is an immediate path to achieving a feeling of self-importance or self-actualization. What would happen, for example, if you cordoned off a small section of the classroom and encouraged children to create a special space just for them—no adults allowed? Given this opportunity to create their own space within the classroom, children will make many choices as they work: what the space will become, the materials and tools to be used, and how it will be assembled. Engaging in the process of making choices, however, gives children much more. It gives them the chance to practice teamwork, negotiation skills, and decision making. It is important to offer plenty of unstructured, open-ended time, which gives children the freedom to make decisions and act upon their ideas.

Another way to promote freedom of choice is to create a classroom schedule in which there are very few times in the day when everyone is doing the same thing at the same time. When children are forced to operate as a large group for the majority of the day, they are merely being herded around or following the leader and, therefore, have few opportunities for making choices.

Here are some additional tips for cultivating children's choices, autonomy, and self-actualization.

- Let them choose a special name for the classroom or areas within it.

- Encourage them to create unique ways of doing ordinary things, such as walking backward holding a friend's hand to go outside.

- Let them decide on classroom rules and expectations.

- Let them establish special classroom traditions, such as bringing a small natural object to school on the first Monday of every month.

- Encourage them to contribute to the classroom by bringing in recycled materials, loose parts, and found natural items.

- Give them opportunities to express their interests through small presentations or showing personal artifacts, such as sharing a rock or button collection with classmates.

Children must be of the opinion that they are important, have value, and have power. They must feel, "I am somebody." Providing environments where children have choices and are actively engaged with both their minds and bodies puts them on the path to self-actualization.

Design Ideas for Choice-Driven Environments

- Give children lots of choices of textured materials that are visually and kinesthetically interesting.

- Reduce the amount of single-use materials, and increase the availability of open-ended materials.

- Organize the environment—especially the shelves—so children can readily see what choices of materials are available.

- Periodically rotate materials so new choices are consistently being offered and highlighted.

- Alert and talk with the children about the new choices available to them.

As early childhood practitioners, our responsibility is to provide environments that meet the basic needs outlined by Maslow as well as continually move children toward their individual self-actualization, which means discovering how to become their best selves. This requires an environment that is safe, healthy, and supportive in which young children can grow to the fullest as happy human beings. We know that children live from moment to moment, rarely thinking of the future, yet they are still learning within these moments. It is our charge to invoke what Maslow calls peak experiences—transcendent moments of pure joy and elation. When we create inspiring spaces, we provide the foundation for children to realize something more than themselves and to seek to manifest their best selves through self-actualization.

Children's Rights in Classroom Design

In the same way that we as adults feel entitled to certain rights, so do children have rights: the right to move as they please, to make decisions with regard to their environment, and to interact with their peers or opt for time by themselves. How might these rights influence classroom design?

Right to Freedom and Movement

Children have a natural instinct to move. Children need autonomy as they learn to navigate the environment. Clutter, congestion, and disorder can hinder children's ability to process and move through the classroom effectively. A space that allows for smooth movement between areas and a natural flow supports a child's independence. Additionally, providing areas with openings that allow children to expand their play into other areas and move without restriction fosters creative freedom. Children need the perceived sense of freedom to grow into competent, autonomous adults.

Right to Autonomy and Competency

As early childhood practitioners, we often think our most important goal is getting children ready for academic success. This is not and should never be our goal; rather, the goal and purpose of early childhood education is to provide classroom experiences that promote children's autonomy and confidence in their competency. Autonomy is a freedom of having choices. It is having the ability to think for oneself, to be independent and self-reliant. Effectively designed classrooms have the potential to support children's competency. Are centers and areas for exploring clearly defined? Are expectations within each area clearly communicated?

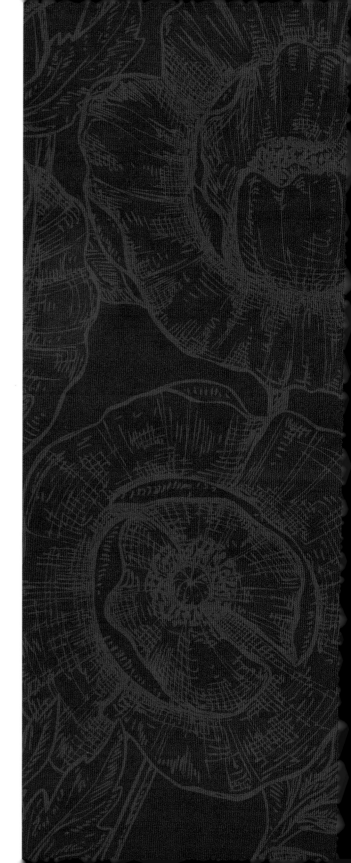

Early childhood author and educator Ann Epstein believes that children's feelings of security and confidence in a space affect the complexity and length of their play. According to Epstein, children feel smaller when in a big space, and they feel large when in a smaller space such as a cozy corner, playhouse, or interest area made for two. The size of a space also affects the quality of the play and potential for learning. If teachers intentionally alter the space to make children feel large in relation to their environments, children may engage in complex play more quickly and may continue the play for longer periods of time. Ultimately, according to Sandra Duncan, classrooms have dispositions—some positive and some not so much. These dispositions affect children's learning.

Children also deserve the right to select where they sit. "Oh sure," you are probably thinking, "But what about Frances, who always pesters the other children if she sits too close to them at story time? And, how on earth do I handle all the kids at group time if they don't have assigned places to sit on the rug? Letting children choose where they sit sounds way too hard. How could I possibly let children decide where to sit?"

In many early childhood classrooms, teachers assign children places where they must sit. It might be a specific chair at the snack table or an identified spot on the rug. Typically, teachers affix laminated labels with the children's names to identify their assigned seats or tape the names on the rug where group meeting is held. Therefore, children do not have a choice of where to sit; they are forced to sit where their name is located regardless of their thoughts or preferences. Although assigned seating might make the teacher's job easier, forcing children to sit in a particular spot takes away their independence, autonomy, and freedom of choice. Give children back their rights as individuals, and allow them to choose where they sit.

Right to Learn through the Senses

Children are wired to be sensory beings. They have little capacity for abstractions. Because of this, children require diverse and varied sensory experiences. Merely talking about the differences in seed pods is not the same as allowing children to actually feel the difference. Children come to understand seed pods only through up-close, personal experiences.

The development of cognitive concepts and sensory awareness begins in infancy and continues throughout life, according to Sandra Duncan and Mickey MacGillivray. Children use their senses to collect data and to formulate their own ideas. Using touch, a child learns about the world through weight, size, temperature, and texture.

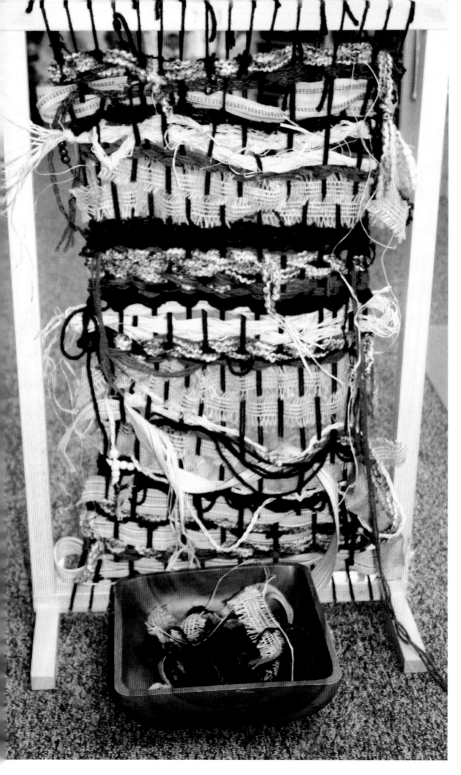

In a well-designed classroom, there is a diversity of materials that offer both visual and tactile experiences. For example, objects from nature come in many textures. Tree pods can be either smooth or rough, sand can be dry or wet, and tree branches can be soft or hard. In all these examples, the tactile processing system interprets information through the touch receptors in the skin. Arranging the classroom environment so that it offers children opportunities for exploring, creating, and learning through their senses must be the main objective of early childhood practitioners. One of the simplest ways to provide sensorial experiences is through hands-on exploration of texture. There are two types of texture: visual and kinesthetic. The following ideas will get you started.

- Find a small end table with two or three drawers. Fill each drawer with a different type of texture, such as bristly, fluffy, and prickly. Encourage children to take out a drawer, explore the objects in it, and return the drawer to the table. Involve children in this kinesthetic experience by asking for suggestions for objects to include.

- Place small braided rugs and soft pillows in secluded areas of the classroom to create a space for one child to be alone.

- Braided table runners add visual texture to the classroom.

- Threading ribbon through chicken wire is a good kinesthetic experience for young children.

- Attach a variety of textured items, such as short chains, brushes, and scouring pads, to a piece of plywood. Place this in the block or manipulative center.

- Ambient lighting and texture play an important role in creating nurturing environments for our psyche. If everything is smooth to the touch or features bright overhead fixtures, we stunt our ability to experience the sensory world around us. By integrating woven textiles and dim lamps or lights, the ability to feel is activated.

- Add wicker placemats and baskets to the construction center's wall décor. They make a statement, are inexpensive, and easy to put up on the wall using double-stick Velcro. Or, simply add woven or wicker placemats to the block area.

Right to Isolation and Socialization

Children have the right to time alone and personal space. They also have the right to have time with friends in community spaces. Traditionally, classrooms have denied the right for a child to choose to isolate and be alone. Think of your own needs; there are invariably times when you need to be alone and in your own space to rest, contemplate, and reflect. Children have the same needs to find space away from busy classroom areas.

Right to Connect with Peers, Families, and Community

Belonging is when children have a connection with their families, peers, and community. Children have a deep need for belonging, as all people do. You can define a community by the shared interests and connections of the people in it. Every classroom has an automatic community comprised of the children, teachers, and families. Fostering this community supports children in feeling a relationship to the classroom and those around them. Try the following ideas to support your classroom community.

- Include photos of the children's families in the classroom.

- Display artifacts or photographs from the local community. Encourage children and their families to take photographs

▼ This cozy place was created using a U-shaped desk. An acrylic mirror was attached to the back side with double-stick tape. A small rug completes the space.

with their cell phones and email them to you. Print out the images and place them in plastic sleeves in a three-ring binder. Place the binder in the block center for children to use as inspiration for their constructions.

- Invite community leaders or experts into the classroom to demonstrate a skill. For example,

- A person who repairs clocks could visit the classroom to share knowledge about how clocks work. Offer old clocks (with glass, electrical cords, and batteries removed) and give children opportunities to tinker, take apart, and put the clocks back together.

- Encourage children and their families to collect natural objects from the local community such as pinecones, wildflowers, river rock, and small twigs to bring into the classroom. Display local artifacts on a table for children to explore.

- Invite children to dig up (with parent or guardian permission) a small amount of dirt from their backyard and put it in a zippered plastic bag to bring to the classroom. Find a large, clear container, and discuss with the children how the container represents their neighborhood. With the children, request that each child pour the soil they dug into the container. Once completed, discuss the differences in texture and color among the types of soil. Be sure to mention how everyone's soil represents your community.

Every person needs a place that is furnished with hope.

—Maya Angelou

Reduce Clatter in the Classroom

Early childhood classrooms are busy, active, and energetic places filled with a cacophony of sounds including children's laughter, conversations, and an occasional skirmish over a favorite toy. There are the sounds of blocks tumbling; music playing; cars and trucks racing up ramps; and dishes, pots, and pans rattling and clattering in the dramatic play corner. While this type of auditory clatter can positively affect children's engagement with the environment and interactions with others, some classrooms are also filled with negative classroom clatter—especially in the physical arrangement of the space.

Clattered environments are mentally and visually noisy and can interrupt children's thought patterns and movements. Although the word *clatter* sounds much like *clutter*, they are not the same. Cluttered classrooms are continually littered with lots of unorganized stuff and are messy and disorganized. Highly cluttered classrooms, nonetheless, can result in clattered classrooms. Both physical and mental clatter results in children being unable to optimally function in the classroom.

Physically Clattered Classroom

A physically noisy, clattered classroom is one that creates physical interruptions to children's movements so they are unable to optimally function in the classroom. There are several problematic design issues that cause a classroom to be physically clattered. For example, an overabundance of furniture or equipment uses valuable square footage and causes cramped spaces, leaving minimal room for children to move about and play. In some cases, overcrowded spaces result in "Alice-in-Wonderland"-type mazes, which create issues for children's navigation of the space. Another example of a physically clattered classroom is one with furniture that is too large for the space available. With every piece of furniture in the classroom, consider the square footage it consumes. If your classroom is filled with large, bulky pieces of furniture, think about how you could substitute a smaller piece of furniture.

Visually Clattered Classroom

Visually noisy classrooms interrupt children's thought patterns; as a result, they are unable to optimally function in the classroom. Examples of visual noise include piles of stuff with no specific purpose and disorganized countertops filled with papers, notes, stuff, and more stuff. Although *clatter* and *clutter* do not mean the same thing, the end results are the same: a dysfunctional classroom.

Declattering	Decluttering
Create clear physical pathways throughout the classroom, including more than one way to get in and out of each center.	Have a pitching party; be ruthless. If you haven't used it in the last two months, it's probably not worth keeping. Throw it away or donate it.
Reduce visual obstructions such as too much stuff hanging from the ceiling or papers taped on the closet door.	If you cannot bear to throw away the stuff, organize it into tubs with lids that can be easily stacked in a closet or on a shelf. Label the tubs so you can quickly find what you are looking for.
Identify the most popular center in the classroom. It should have the greatest amount of square footage devoted to it. Make centers large enough so children have enough room to freely navigate within the space. .	Tackle the obvious clutter first, which is the stuff right before your very eyes—you know, areas such as the art cart or paint-drying rack with children's pictures from two months ago. Make a vow to yourself to keep the area tidy and organized.
Critically think about each piece of furniture in your classroom and ask yourself: • Do I need this? • Do the children use it? • What would happen if I got rid of it? If the answers are no, no, and nothing, then remove the piece of furniture from the classroom. It is serving no purpose.	Identify the clutter magnets—these are areas where clutter likes to go, such as storage cabinets, drawers, and closets. Spend time keeping these areas free of clutter.
	Have a clutter goal. For example, commit to throwing out a grocery bag—or better yet, a large garbage bag—full of stuff.

Visual Thinking

Visual thinking is the interaction among seeing, thinking, understanding, and doing. It's the combination of using our eyes and minds. According to Stanford University professor Robert McKim, the habits of seeing and thinking are intimately related.

Children learn with all five of their senses, but the sense of sight is an important but often underestimated variable in the classroom. Early childhood environments are typically filled with a plethora of visual images, which often become visual clutter or noise. Most of these images, such as posters, signs, pictures, and words on labels, are posted by teachers with the mistaken notion that seeing is knowing. Simply seeing does not automatically result in children's understanding of what they see. Rather, children's understanding begins when the posted images promote visual thinking and visual attention.

Briefly put down this book and focus on a nearby object in your immediate environment, such as a chair, coffee cup, or flower vase. Stare at the object and try to filter out everything around, under, behind, or over the object. Concentrate on seeing the object—nothing else. Now pretend the object is resting on a black background, and once again attempt to filter out the space and things around the object. Ignore your peripheral vision. Stare fixedly at the object with its black background and attempt to visually grasp this shape by itself and nothing else. Could you do it? If not, was it frustrating? If so, was it challenging? If you are like most people, it was probably impossible to exclude or block out everything surrounding the chosen object. Consider the following lessons that can be learned from this visual-attention experience.

- Keeping undivided attention on the same object for any length of time requires finding something new or interesting about it, such as a chip in a flower vase, a drop of moisture on the coffee cup, or a snag in the chair's fabric.

- Focusing without distractions is virtually impossible.

▼ This child's clay sculpture is reflective of *visual thinking*, which is defined as the combination of using our eyes and minds.

What does this mean for early childhood classrooms? If adults find this visual thinking exercise difficult, then undoubtedly young children find it challenging to focus their attention. Young children's attention spans are certainly shorter than adults. According to early childhood expert Pam Schiller, on average, an adult's attention maxes out at about seventeen minutes of attention compared to children, who have one minute of attention span per year of age plus one. Therefore, a child who is three years old has an attention span of four minutes, and a four-year-old has an attention span of five minutes. With that knowledge, we should consider strategies for reducing obstacles in the early childhood environment that can interfere with children's visual focus. Try the following strategies for increasing children's visual thinking and attention.

- **Reduce visual background noise.** An easy strategy for creating environments that promote visual thinking is to design an environment with minimal visual background noise. For example, select window coverings that are made with plain or minimally patterned fabric. Use natural backgrounds on bulletin boards, such as burlap or brown butcher paper, and select natural materials, such as wicker or bamboo for bulletin-board borders.

- **Keep the patterns simple.** Our brains have an innate urge to seek order out of chaos, so it's best to eliminate squiggly lines or complex designs and patterns on walls and floors. Instead, consider integrating natural-looking swirls and waves, which can be very calming and easy on the eyes. Even though most of nature's motifs are asymmetrical, it's the repeating aspect of these elements that add serenity to a space.

▲ Children's images are the focal point of this classroom. Their beautiful faces and active hands illustrate the classroom's work and energy.

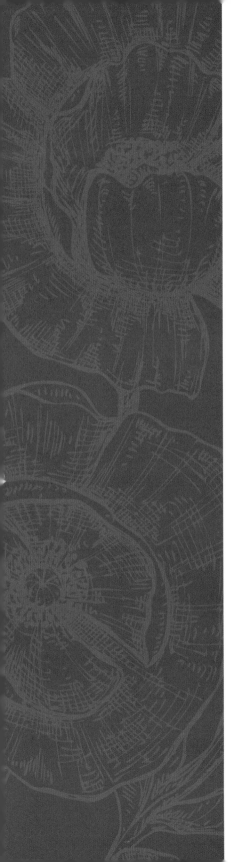

- **Choose items intentionally.** Limit the amount of stuff posted on walls or hanging from the classroom's ceilings. Have a specific purpose for everything posted, and be finicky about what you choose. Be sure to post materials that have a meaningful context for children. They should be able to understand what the item is, what it means, and why it is there. Draw different colored shapes on large index cards with the name of the color written below the shapes in both English and Spanish. A red square will have the words *red* and *rojo* written right below it. Place the cards in the literacy or math center for children to enjoy.

- **Clump posted materials together in a way that makes sense with surrounding space.** For example, hang children's drawings of flowers in the science center rather than in the block corner. In the block corner, post images related to construction, engineering, and buildings or structures. Keep cabinet and classroom doors free of paper and posted materials.

- **Cut the cute.** It is a common practice for teachers to purchase commercially made alphabet posters for the early childhood classroom. Teachers often select cutesy versions that combine a letter of the alphabet along with an image representing the letter. For example, a poster might have the lowercase letter *r* with an image of a rabbit holding the *r*, three carrots, some dirt, the word *rabbit*, and arrows illustrating how to draw the letter. There are several issues with this type of poster: The child may think the image is of a bunny, which totally upsets the apple cart because *bunny* begins with the letter *b*. The child needs to visually filter out all the extra lines and images to focus on the letter *r* in order for the poster to be effective. This may be very challenging for many young children.

- **Infuse freshness to spark visual thinking.** If we want to keep children's attention and increase visual thinking, then it is important to design environments that offer fresh and interesting objects. This means selecting extraordinary objects to foster children's discoveries and spark aha moments. Visual thinking is an act of continual discovery. Children's discovery and attention expands when the visual environment is rich and when objects in the environment are new and original to the mind.

Stagnant and unoriginal materials do not stimulate children's visual thinking. Sadly, early childhood classrooms are often stagnant in the display of materials. Block corners, for example, are often set up with blocks, transportation signs, cars and trucks, and so on; many teachers do not give the area another thought. Think about the block corner in your classroom. When is the last time you freshened it with new and original objects?

▲ Working on vertical learning surfaces, such as this metal wall, helps children develop spatial awareness and learn basic spatial concepts, such as left, right, up, down, high, and low.

▲ There is too much information for children to process in this classroom. A simple fix would be reducing the number of pictures on the wall to make more white space.

The View on the Walls

Early childhood environments are busy, active, and energetic places filled with visual overload—especially on classroom walls. It is not uncommon to see bulletin boards with busily designed, scalloped borders and brightly colored backgrounds scattered throughout the space. There are multitudes of posters in a variety of primary colors filled with information such as the alphabet, classroom rules, handwashing steps, calendar, colors, and shapes. Children's unframed artwork is stapled or taped to the walls. Notices to families, along with reminder notes for the staff and a plethora of mandatory postings for licensing or accreditation, also cover the surfaces of the walls and the cabinet fronts and doors.

Posting many things on the walls is traditionally accepted, which means many teachers believe filling the walls with posters or paper is the appropriate way to decorate the classroom. This visual stimulation can overwhelm children. Children's senses are designed to detect changes in stimulation rather than to monitor a steady input of stimuli. When designing environments for young children, it's a matter of having neither too much nor too little stimulation. Instead, find just the right amount. For example, dramatic fluctuations in stimulation can be disorienting to young children, but moderately diverse patterns of stimulation help children maintain optimal levels of responsiveness and positive feelings of being comfortable. Moderately diverse stimulation can be beneficial to young children as it promotes children's optimal behaviors, stimulates their interests, and encourages positive responses.

Young children are learning the cognitive skill known as *information processing*. Information processing allows us to see, process, and then interpret meaning from what we see. When there is too much visual information for young children to process, they become overwhelmed and frustrated. Frustration inevitably leads to negative behavior. Fortunately, it is easy to solve this problem in the classroom environment. To build children's information-processing skills, reduce the amount of information they must process. Use the following ideas and tips to help reduce the amount of visual stimulation in your classroom.

- **Create white space between pictures on the walls.** This strategy gives pictures and objects breathing space and allows children's eyes to focus and process the information.

- **Design visual balance between objects on the wall.** Visual balance helps children know what is important and what is unimportant. Visual cues help the brain organize thinking, remember information, and increase engagement. Visual balance allows children's eyes to rest, while imbalance overwhelms and distracts. Our eyes need rest.

For many young children, visual overload from a classroom filled with clutter on the walls creates stress and discomfort. The well-intentioned posters and charts become nothing more than visual noise because most children have a hard time knowing where to look, so they try to filter out the noisy walls. Filtering or ignoring, however, is challenging and next to impossible, as most young children do not have the ability to process visual overload and to filter out excessive stimuli. Children with sensory-processing issues have an especially hard time engaging in overstimulating environments.

As educators and architects of classrooms, it is our responsibility to break the traditional aesthetic code of "more is better." As Sandra Duncan and Jody Martin assert in their book *Rethinking the Classroom Landscape*, this means, "decluttering the walls, removing commercially produced materials, and placing children's framed creative expressions, as well as thoughtfully chosen masterpieces, such as Monet or Rembrandt throughout the classroom." By doing so, teachers can begin to honor children's work and create beautiful spaces.

Be Creative in Your Displays

Making meaningful connections is the foundation of all learning. Our brains are wired to make connections between what we know and what we are experiencing or learning at the moment. If the classroom's walls are cluttered with materials that bear no relationship to children's learning or do not reflect the children's lives and cultures, then it becomes difficult for them to make meaningful connections. The challenge is to discard the notion of decorating your classroom walls and, instead, to consider how you can effectively use the walls to convey the curriculum and learning objectives. More importantly, consider the walls as a reflection of the children who are in the classroom every day. Ask yourself the following questions before posting materials on classroom walls.

- What is the purpose of the material that I am posting?

- Who is the audience for this material: children, families, visitors?

- Are the materials that I am posting honoring children's work, as opposed to posting commercially purchased materials that are unrelated to the work of the classroom?

- Are the materials a reflection of the children's cultures, families, or community?

- Are the materials interactive or passive? If passive, how can I make the materials more interactive?

To reduce wall clutter, consider the following strategies.

- Reduce commercially purchased posters by 50 percent. Rather than hanging every child's picture on the wall, create a three-ring binder with clear plastic sleeves for children to display their work. Children will enjoy putting in (and taking out) their work and will get to view the art of other classmates. Place the binder with the children's work in the library or near the sign in/out area so that everyone can enjoy the artwork.

- Instead of hanging children's artwork on the walls, find other places to display it such as framed pictures on tops of shelves.

- Hang clipboards on the wall near the art or writing center. Encourage children to post their work on the clipboards.

- Purchase a roll of cork (available at craft stores), and cut a variety of sizes and shapes, all of which will accommodate an 8 1/2" x 11" piece of paper. With heavy-duty glue, affix a large clothespin to the top of the cork shape. Then affix the cork shape to the wall with double-stick tape near the art or writing area.

- Placemats provide a great way to frame children's work or required information for families. Simply sew or glue a small ribbon to the back of the placemat and use the ribbon for hanging the placemat on the wall.

- A digital photo frame is a great way to display children's artwork—especially in an area where both family members and children can see it. Take pictures of children's work with a camera or smartphone, download the images to your computer, and either save them on a USB stick or download the images straight from your computer.

- If your computer has PowerPoint, create a slideshow with images of children's work (and even pictures of children actively involved in a project). There is a function in PowerPoint that allows the slide show to repeat. Set up your computer in a safe but easily visible area, and press "start slideshow." Using the same idea, you can take videos of children at work and download the video to a PowerPoint slide presentation.

Rethink Bulletin Boards

Bulletin boards are a common staple in most early childhood classrooms. Teachers use them in a variety of ways, including displaying children's projects and artwork; recognizing holidays and seasons; posting calendars and weather charts; informing families of upcoming events or announcements; and displaying curriculum materials such as the alphabet, colors, and shapes. Too often, however, bulletin boards are only thought of as room decoration or a place to display children's artwork. According to educator and author Michael Gravois, bulletin boards can be more than décor—they can be a learning and teaching tool or a way to reinforce instructional goals. Here are two ways to actively involve children with the bulletin boards in your classroom.

Let the Children Choose the Content

The key to making bulletin boards a learning tool is not just in the board's content but in the creation of the board itself. Give children a sense of ownership in the classroom by allowing them to make decisions about what will be on the board and also contribute to the board's contents. Children can paint, write, and gather the necessary materials as well as assist in assembling the board.

▲ This adorable toddler is creating a bulletin board with curlers, which easily adhere to the felt backing of the board.

Make Them Interactive

Position a bulletin board at children's eye level so it is easily accessible for them. Then create fun and engaging activities for children to do on the board. For example, have children match baby animals with their mothers, such as a cow and calf, or dress the community helpers with appropriate gear, such as a firefighter and fire helmet. A variety of materials, such as felt, Pellon, and paper, can be used to make the pieces that children manipulate. If paper is used for the pieces, be sure to laminate them for durability. Felt-backed pieces will stick to the board if it is covered with fabric or felt. Double-stick Velcro, magnetic tape, or Pellon also work well as sticking materials. Pellon, which is an interfacing fabric used in sewing and can be purchased at fabric stores, is ideal. Because it is lightweight, you can trace objects or characters from a storybook onto it, and you can color it with permanent marker. Once cut out, the pieces are perfect for an interactive bulletin board.

Bulletin boards can be an effective furnishing for the early childhood classroom if their contents are designed with purpose and intentionality. Avoid bright primary-colored backgrounds or patterned borders. These kinds of materials compete with and take away from the beauty of children's artwork. Cartoon-type characters or seasonally decorated borders have little relevance to the classroom's work, so don't use them. Instead, cover the boards with plain fabric, felt, or burlap in earth tones. An advantage to covering the board in fabric is that it won't fade as easily as construction or bulletin-board paper. Rather than using commercially purchased borders, create borders with natural colors and simple textures. A border of thin sticks or twigs can surround the board. Use placemats and plate chargers to frame children's work. Here are ideas for simple and inexpensive bulletin board materials.

Background and Border Ideas	Affixing Ideas	Authentic Materials
• Burlap	• Double-stick Velcro	• Placemats
• Fabric	• Magnetic tape	• Table runners
• Wallpaper pieces	• Removable strips	• Tree cookies (cross sections of trees)
• Felt	• Pellon interfacing	• Sticks
• Wide ribbon	• Sticky putty	• Picture frames
• Cork squares	• Adhesive paper	• Leaves or dried flowers

You can also use bulletin boards to communicate with families. Aim to develop boards with a goal in mind, such as informing families about the daily or weekly lesson plans, daily schedule, teachers' schedules, field trip information, menus, or family newsletters. Include a place for family members to share information or ask questions. One idea is to cover a tissue box with a plainly designed wrapping paper and affix it to the board. You may want to provide small sheets of paper and miniature pencils (golf pencils work great) so family members can communicate with you. Finally, whatever is included on the family bulletin must be neatly done and consistently updated.

Criteria for Effective Bulletin Boards

- Relevant
- Simple
- Appealing
- Purposeful
- Understandable
- Current
- Functional

- Attractive
- Interactive
- Personalized
- Neutral colors
- Community-focused
- Authentic materials

If you don't have a bulletin board or the funds to purchase one, make one by covering a large piece of cardboard with fabric or bulletin board paper and suspending it from the ceiling using metal hooks. It's lightweight and easy to hang.

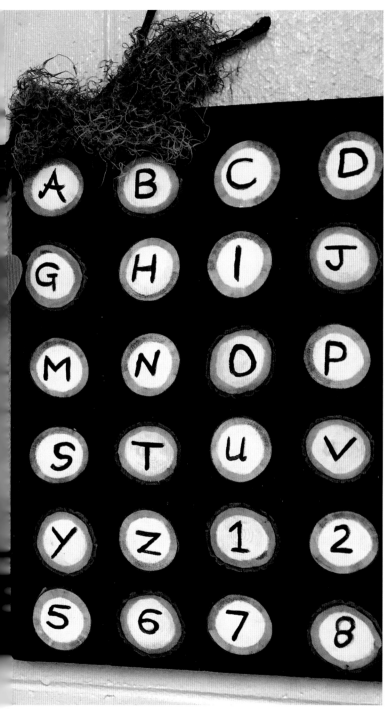

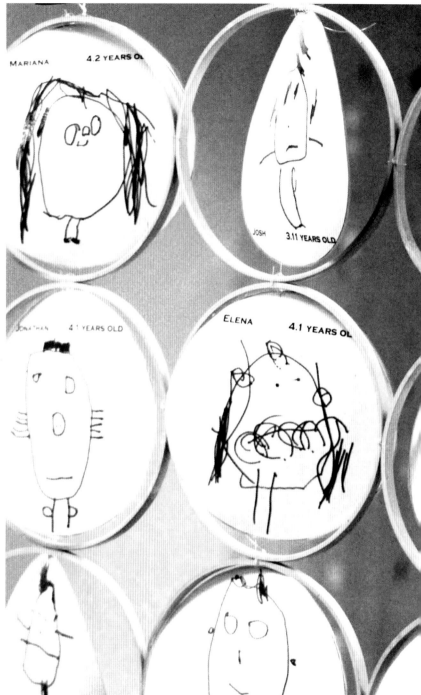

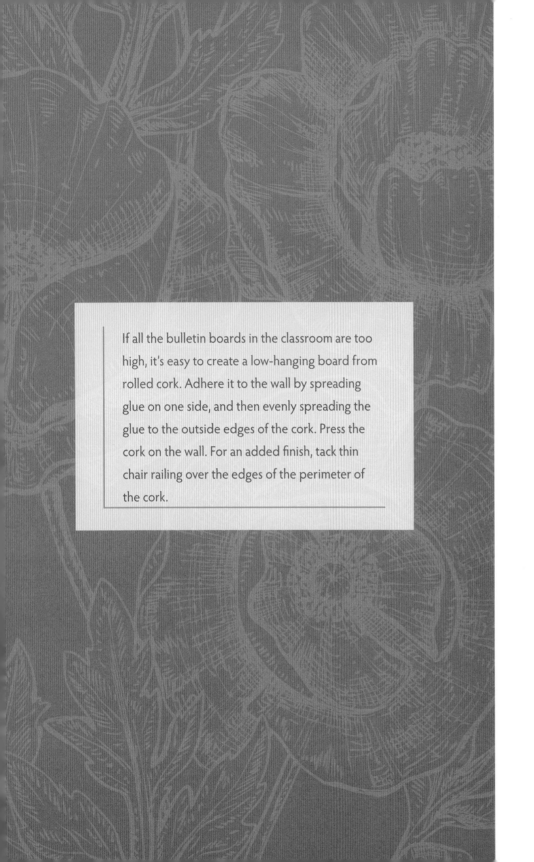

If all the bulletin boards in the classroom are too high, it's easy to create a low-hanging board from rolled cork. Adhere it to the wall by spreading glue on one side, and then evenly spreading the glue to the outside edges of the cork. Press the cork on the wall. For an added finish, tack thin chair railing over the edges of the perimeter of the cork.

The National Association for the Education of Young Children (NAEYC), one of the largest advocates for children in the country, emphasizes that classroom materials should spark children's interests. NAEYC also recommends that young children's environments be organized and well-maintained to facilitate learning across all learning domains. NAEYC's criteria for center accreditation requires that children's work be displayed at eye level, for teachers to create classroom displays to help children reflect on and extend their learning, and that children's recent works—art, emergent writing, graphic representation, and three-dimensional creations— be predominant in classroom displays. NAEYC's definition of *predominant* is that more than 50 percent of the displays are child created. Remember, though, that more is not always better when it comes to displaying in an early childhood environment.

▲ Cluster objects hanging from the ceiling in groups of three, five, or seven.

The View from the Ceiling

Have you ever found a comfortable patch of grass on a beautiful day, lay down, and watched the billowy white clouds float gently through the crystal blue sky? Watching clouds in a gorgeous summer sky can be quite peaceful, but when the storm clouds gather and the sky becomes menacing, cloud watching is no longer peaceful.

▲ Child-painted pinecones hung with braided thread on a small tree branch make an ideal three-dimensional object to hang from the ceiling.

At times, classroom ceilings are a bit like a sky filled with storm clouds. Just like the rumbling clouds prior to a summer storm, there is a lot of stuff rumbling about on the classroom ceiling: fixtures, emergency lighting, ceiling tiles, fluorescent lights, sprinkler heads, air vents, heat and smoke detectors, exit signs, security cameras, and sometimes speakers or intercom systems. In addition to all these essential or required items, there may be items such as mobiles, paper lanterns, signs designating learning centers, children's projects, twigs and branches, draped fabric, and seasonal items such as holiday garland and construction-paper autumn leaves or flowers. When you think about it, that's a lot of visual stimuli that young children have to decipher—either by processing, ignoring, or reacting. Because we know that children can only attend to one thing at a time, the idea of processing everything on the ceiling is probably not going to happen. That leaves two choices for children: ignore or react. If children end up ignoring, then we need to ask ourselves whether something should necessarily be hung from the ceiling. If children end up reacting, then the result could be a negative response and may include acting-out behaviors because the children are unable to assimilate or filter out the overwhelming stimuli.

So, what's a teacher to do? Is hanging nothing from the ceiling the answer? Probably not. If items are hung from the ceiling in a thoughtful way, then the positioning of these items will make sense to young children. If items are intentionally selected and purposefully hung, then children can make meaning and understand them.

There are three reasons for hanging items from the ceiling: identifying a learning area, bringing attention to an area, and creating a focal point. Whatever you hang must draw children to the area.

Although everything hanging from the ceiling must have a specific and valid reason for being there, an equally important requirement is to be sure what you hang from the ceiling connects with what is below it. In other words, a mobile made with a bunch of silverware utensils is inappropriate for the science area but is very much connected to the home living space. An empty lampshade hanging over the home living table is appropriate in this area, but doesn't necessarily connect in the block corner.

Depending on the size of the objects, a general rule of thumb is to limit hanging items to no more than three. Hanging more than three items in a normal-sized classroom could cause visual overload. Be sure that there is plenty of visual space between hangings by suspending them in separate parts of the room. To create a visual (but invisible) horizontal line, hang all items the same distance from the floor so objects are on the same visual plane. For example, if you are hanging a large tree branch with the end approximately seven feet from the floor, be sure to hang the paper lanterns so the bottoms of the lanterns are also seven feet from the floor. Hang the objects low enough so children can see them and enjoy them, but realize that small and thin objects are not visually interesting when viewed from below. Three-dimensional objects work best.

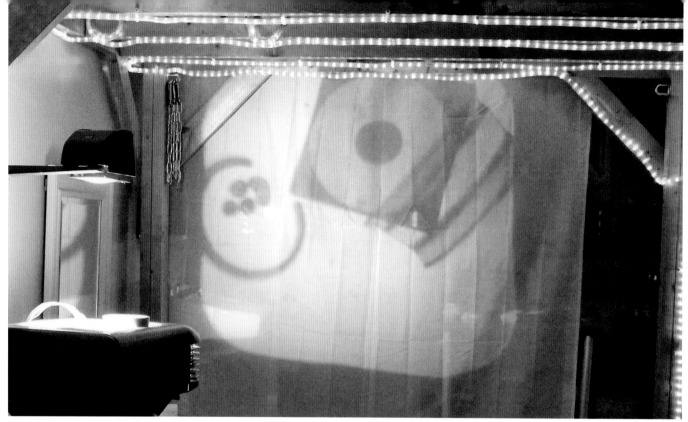

▲ Projecting images on a sheet or white piece of thin cloth with an overhead projector stimulates children's visual thinking.

Items hanging from the classroom ceiling can be more for the adults' gratification than the children's benefit. For example, think about center signs with words such as *Block, Art*, and *Science* that often hang from the ceiling over interest centers denoting the areas. Even if the center signs include pictures reflecting the kinds of materials found in each area, children are not likely to look up to observe, extrapolate meaning, or understand what the signage says before entering that area. Similarly, all the precut commercial decorative images of themes, such as community helpers, transportation, plants, and seasons, go unnoticed if they are not at the child's eye level. These may also become visual clutter if left hanging from the ceiling too long. And what do these images teach anyway? Maybe nothing if the ceiling objects are not meaningful to the child's world.

Perhaps what's hanging from the ceiling isn't as important as how it is hung from the ceiling. For example, draping chiffon, tulle, or some twinkle lights in a back corner projects a sense of calm and peacefulness, which may invite children to come into this area for some alone or quiet time. Placing colorful designs in odd numbers—one, three, or five items—with the surface side hanging down may inspire children in the art area. Projecting abstract images in muted colors on the ceiling during naptime may help children relax. Allowing children to decorate ceiling tiles and placing the tiles above the children may offer objects for contemplation and comfort during rest time.

Ceiling Views for Infants

What adults see is strikingly different from what infants see. Consider, for example, a mobile hanging from the ceiling. Because adults see the mobile from its side, they are able to enjoy it from an overall perspective; however, babies on the floor looking up may only see the bottom of the mobile. If the mobile is primarily made from two-dimensional materials, such as fabric strips or construction paper, the baby will see only the underside of the material. Mobiles constructed with three-dimensional objects provide the most benefit for infants. Consider the following tips for improving ceiling views for infants.

- Use lightweight fabric that will move when someone passes by or when the heater or air-conditioning fan starts up. The swirling movement of the fabric will catch the infant's eye.

- Add three-dimensional objects that also have the capacity for sound, such as bells or wind chimes, or kitchen utensils such as spoons or whisks.

- Include LED lights on the mobile for visual interest.

- Hang the mobile low enough for infants to see. **Safety note:** Make sure mobiles are securely hung.

Three-Dimensional Mobile Objects that Make Sound

- Metal utensils
- Keys
- Seashells
- Doorknobs
- Wire birdhouses
- Paper lanterns
- Wind chimes
- Large bells
- Driftwood
- Costume jewelry
- Pie tins
- Chains

6

Authenticity: Infusing Everyday Objects into the Classroom

Children actively explore their environment by using their senses to learn and understand the world around them. Young children learn best through interactive engagement and play in a high-quality learning environment filled with authentic materials, resources, and equipment. Authenticity in the classroom is the presence of materials and resources that are used in the real world for real purposes. Everyday authentic objects provide rich sensory information necessary for young children's learning and development, so they are a perfect addition to the early childhood classroom.

Sensory Exploration with Traditional versus Authentic Materials

When selecting toys, equipment, and learning materials for young children, consider the sensorial input of these objects. The classroom should be filled with sensorial opportunities—especially visual and kinesthetic. Classrooms are typically filled with traditional toys purchased from a catalog, neighborhood garage sale, or local retailer. The majority of these toys are made from plastic. The sensory input of plastic toys is minimal because most plastic is smooth to the touch, so it has little kinesthetic-learning value. Kinesthetic learning occurs when children learn through their sense of feel. In other words, those children that are tactile learners and prefer to learn about their environment through hands-on learning would not benefit from this type of toy. Not only is there a lack of texture to feel, but

▲ Children will be immediately curious about an old typewriter and how it works.

▲ Pretend

▲ Authentic

most plastic surfaces have little visual interest or texture to see either. Visual texture is when the objects children are seeing have a great deal of visual differences, such as grooves, bumps, ridges, and concave areas. For example, think about the sensory differences between a real phone versus a plastic toy phone purchased from a toy catalog. A school system located in the Midwest purchased classroom plastic phones at a cost of almost fifty dollars per phone. Because the children did not play with them, one of the teachers decided to scout around the community and look for real telephones for the children's home living area.

The commercially purchased make-believe play phones were replaced with the real phones purchased at a local thrift shop for two dollars each. The teacher noticed that the children played with the real phones every day. Why? First, the real phone had much more weight to it than the plastic phone. The real phone also had different textures and materials: smooth receiver, bumpy front piece, and a stretchy wire cord, which were all elements for intricate sensory engagement and exploration for the young children.

▲ Pretend

Imagine the child's experience of eating from the plastic dish set from a school supply company versus pretend eating from a real wooden plate setting on a woven placemat with a cloth napkin and acrylic glass.

The plastic tea set has one distinct quality--it is plastic. The metal tea pot has a very cool metal feeling as well as weight and has visual texture and depth with its markings, indentations, and engravings.

Authentic everyday objects provide curiosity and interest. Take a close look at a commercially purchased house set equipped with an oven, stove, sink, and cabinets. There's nothing dramatically wrong with it. It's a housekeeping set typically seen in many early childhood classrooms, with lots of primary colors and plenty of plastic. Imagine how children would use that piece of equipment in a home living area. Now imagine how children would construct their learning in this home living area using authentic objects such as real dishes, a tablecloth, a table centerpiece, and a real storage cabinet.

These authentic items create interest for children because they are more intriguing than pretend play objects. The more authentic the materials, the more powerful the engagement.

▲ Authentic

Rich sensory objects encourage children's growth and development across all learning domains and the five senses. Some things may be interesting to see or touch because of the color and texture of the surface. Some items, such as a flower or cinnamon stick, may have a delightful smell. And there are those items that have auditory properties when they are shaken or tapped. Some items, such as fresh berries, have many of these sensory properties, but the best property is their sweet taste.

Any object that stimulates the sense of touch is considered a sensory material. As children handle real everyday objects, their senses experience concepts such as heavy and light, skinny and fat, and smooth and bumpy. By manipulating real objects, children also visually learn critical math concepts such as short and long, alike and different, more and less, and tall and short. A classroom with authentic materials provides young children opportunities to expand their oral language and vocabulary as they learn new words to describe what they are exploring—colors, textures, weight, and size.

▲ A colorful scarf acts as a small tablecloth. Perched on top of the tablecloth are authentic objects including a teapot, colander, and wood cutting board.

▲ This charming home-living area includes a variety of authentic objects combined with a few plastic objects.

Psychologist and child-development expert Jean Piaget believed that when children are playing or engaging in the physical properties of objects, they are constructing a mental model of their world. Children learn best through authentic mental models of their world. To discover the types of mental models children experience in your classroom, make a list of the authentic items in each of the learning centers. It takes a rich variety of authentic materials to provide deeply satisfying play for children. Walk through your classroom and take a close look at each center. For each item in a center, ask yourself, "Is this a reproduction of a real object? Could I replace it with a safe real object?" In the home living center, determine whether or not 50 percent or more of the materials and objects are authentic. Then, look around your classroom and determine what you have that is plastic and could be replaced with authentic items. Once you have determined which areas could use more authenticity, you can start looking for interesting, new, original items to add that will spark the children's curiosity and imagination.

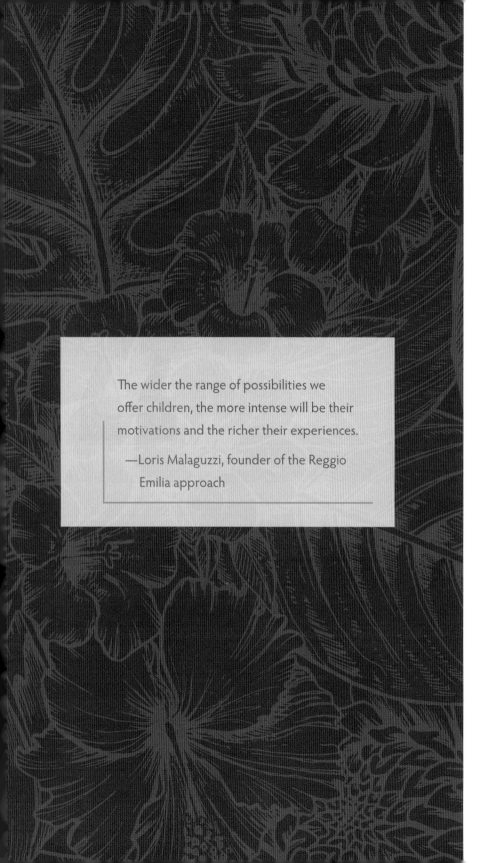

> The wider the range of possibilities we offer children, the more intense will be their motivations and the richer their experiences.
>
> —Loris Malaguzzi, founder of the Reggio Emilia approach

Authenticity with Loose Parts

Architect Simon Nicholson coined the term *loose parts*. Nicholson believed the availability and use of loose parts was an important component of creativity and higher-order thinking. Loose parts are any collection of natural or man-made objects that can be used to extend and further ideas in children's play and construction. According to Nicholson, loose parts are any type of open-ended materials that can be moved, combined, taken apart, redesigned, lined up, restructured, and more. Since there is no predetermined use or preconceived function of loose parts, they are entirely open to a child's interpretation and creative thinking. Think of loose parts as the pathway for children of all ages to unlock their cognitive and creative mindset. With open-ended loose parts, children unleash their inherent powers of creativity and work together to build, construct, and create.

Fostering 21st-Century Thinking Skills

It is our responsibility to begin preparing young children to become productive citizens who will make positive contributions to their communities and workplaces. Over the past few years, the skills needed to be successful in the workforce have changed appreciably—and will continue to change at breakneck speed.

Today's workplace is permeated with technology that enables rapid communication and networking abilities across the globe. Tomorrow's workplace will include even more advanced technologies, such as virtual reality and robotics, allowing teams to work together simultaneously on projects while residing in offices across the world. With this incredible infusion of technology, it is critical to prepare today's children to be future workers with technological skills. Although technical knowledge will continue to be essential, many workforce-trend experts assert that a new group of skills is emerging. These emerging skills include innovation, problem solving, flexibility, and creativity—and are known as the *creative economy*.

Loose parts offer children infinite play and construction opportunities, which ultimately influence their abilities to think and work creatively. Because loose parts are open ended and allow children to do the thinking, the immense benefits of offering loose-parts exploration is critical to development of the next generation. Using loose parts encourages children to become thinkers at a deep level and promotes an intricate process of problem solving. The parts' unique aspects result in children's intense persistence and engagement.

The most remarkable advantage of loose parts is their ability to seamlessly align with both the children's age and their skill levels. No matter the age or ability, children can explore with the same materials and use them in different ways according to their age development, skills, and—most importantly—interest levels.

Loose parts also promote a wide variety of play behaviors including social play, dramatic play, constructive play, symbolic play, and even games with rules. Because loose parts have no predetermined expectations, children can easily make up their own games and accompanying rules with a variety of loose materials.

Creativity is for the gifted few: the rest of us are compelled to live in environments constructed by the gifted few, listen to the gifted few's music, use the gifted few's inventions and art, and read the poems, fantasies, and plays by the gifted few. This is what our education and culture conditions us to believe, and this is a culturally induced and perpetuated lie.

—Simon Nicholson, "How Not to Cheat Children: The Theory of Loose Parts"

Seven Types of Loose Parts

After understanding the need for loose parts, many teachers ask, "Where do I begin?" Begin by looking around your garage, attic, or basement. Find objects children might enjoy exploring. Sort the objects by the different types of textures or materials such as woven, wicker, metal, and fabric. Many of these objects may be a perfect addition to your classroom's environment and provide rich opportunities for exploration and discovery. Not only are found objects free, they are often recyclable and come from easy-to-obtain materials. Loose parts come in an infinite variety of material types. Often, they have a history. Knowing the different characteristics of shape, texture, color, and form will help you figure out how to bring these materials into the classroom.

Safety note: Keep safety in mind when choosing loose parts, and select materials appropriate for the children's age and skill level.

Seven Types of Loose Parts

1. Nature based
- Leaves
- Dirt or sand
- Twigs
- Seashells
- Pinecones
- Driftwood
- Rocks
- Moss
- Tree cookies
- Acorns
- Logs
- Seed pods from trees
- Fruit pits
- Squash
- Feathers
- Sweet gum balls
- Anise stars
- Cattails
- Flowers
- Gourds
- Sea sponges
- Tree bark
- Granite
- Slate

2. Recyclable wood
- Table legs
- Chair legs
- Spools and dowels
- Frames
- Game pieces
- Paint stirrers
- Clothespins
- Wooden pegs
- Puzzle pieces
- Wooden rings
- Wooden napkin rings
- Hardwood floor scraps
- Wooden candlesticks
- Corks
- Golf tees
- Cutting boards
- Wooden bowls
- Dominoes
- Crates
- Small drawers

3. Plastic
- PVC Pipes
- CD cases
- Straws
- Bag clips
- Large plastic hoops
- Golf balls
- Cups
- Beads
- Bottle caps
- Funnels
- Six-pack rings
- Buttons
- Lollipop sticks
- Bubble wrap
- Cones
- Curtain rings
- Hair rollers
- Film canisters
- TV-dinner trays
- Formula containers
- Empty spice containers
- Small cups

4. Metal
- Curtain rings
- Bangles and bells
- Aluminum foil
- Nuts and bolts
- Potato masher
- License plates
- Soda-can tabs and juice-can lids
- Locks and keys
- Silverware and cutlery
- Tin cans
- Hubcaps
- Candlestick holders
- Bobby pins
- Doorknobs
- Measuring cups
- Thimbles
- Tiaras
- Chains
- Screens
- Keyrings
- Magnets
- Metal lids
- Muffin and baking tins

5. Ceramics and glass
- Beads
- Prisms
- Gems
- Marbles
- Coffee cups
- Sea glass
- Disco ball
- Mirrors
- Drawer knobs
- Tiny bottles
- Mason jars
- Ceramic cups
- Vases
- Bottles
- Flower pots
- Ceramic tiles
- Plates
- Baby-food jars
- China

6. Fabric and ribbon
- Pipe cleaners
- Terry cloth
- Velvet
- Corduroy
- Tulle
- Scarves
- Silk
- Wool
- Ribbon
- Twine
- Chiffon
- Embroidery thread
- Burlap
- String
- Lace
- Doilies
- Felt
- Thread
- Rope
- Yarn
- Zip ties
- Raffia

7. Packaging materials
- Duct tape
- Packing tape
- Labels
- Corks
- Cardboard
- Raffia
- Packing peanuts
- Tissue paper
- Paper scraps
- Cereal boxes
- Ribbon wheel
- Egg cartons
- Paper-towel-tube rolls
- Gift boxes
- Bubble wrap
- Cellophane
- Shredded paper
- Magazine pages
- Newspaper
- Styrofoam
- Wrapping paper
- Cardboard boxes

▲ Natural items are great to have children gather on walks and in backyards. Nature-based objects can also include items made out of natural materials, such as wicker baskets, wooden bowls, or wicker woven placemats.

▲ Buttons are terrific loose parts and can be used for classification, categorization, and even works of art. Many households have spare buttons hanging around, so a simple request to parents will yield lots of interesting buttons of various colors, shapes, and sizes.

▲ Metal comes in many forms, sizes, and textures. From the simplicity of nuts and bolts to the complexity of a bicycle wheel, metal offers kinesthetic experiences that are rich and varied in texture. Metal objects often have a reflective surface and more weight. A good and inexpensive source for metal is an automobile junkyard.

Finding Authentic Everyday Objects

The most challenging obstacle is changing our mindset and perceptions about the objects we encounter every day. An easy way to begin is to start looking for interesting items. One of the most wonderful things about loose parts and upcycled materials is that they can be acquired for little to no cost. Look in nature, your home, thrift stores, garage sales, recycle shops, a neighbor's garage, a relative's basement—or on the side of the street on garbage pick-up day. It's not about spending money on new things but about having eyes for old, reusable, and recyclable materials. There is a multitude of ways to find authentic treasures to use in your classroom. Next time you are out and about, think about what items you could add.

One of the best ways to collect authentic everyday objects is to ask the families of your students. Many families cannot afford to contribute money to class projects but may easily offer unused items. Including families in the collection of desired items brings a sense of community and partnership between home and the classroom.

▲ A discarded wine rack creates an open-ended invitation for play and construction.

Getting donations from families is one of the most powerful sources for materials. Send home a letter with your top needs.

Dear Families,

We are collecting the following items for our classroom. Please check around your home, garage, basement, and attic for any unused items you are willing to donate.

Thank you!

- fabric tablecloth
- fabric napkins
- woven placemats
- candlesticks
- vases
- old microwave
- old toaster oven
- old telephone
- hand beaters
- funnels

- mixing bowls
- baskets
- wooden bowls
- wooden spoons
- typewriter
- adding machine
- cash register
- plates, bowls, cups
- aquarium
- wooden shelf

- wooden bench
- ottoman
- sheer curtains
- neutral curtains
- chip and dip plate
- kitchen scale
- measuring cups
- side table
- coffee table

Nature is imperfectly perfect, filled with loose parts and possibilities, with mud and dust, nettles and sky, transcendent hands-on moments and skinned knees.

—Richard Louv, *Last Child in the Woods*

Garage or tag sales are wonderful places to find all sorts of treasures. You can find almost anything on your list. The biggest challenge is the time it takes to travel from one garage sale location to the next. Finding neighborhood-wide garage sales is a good way to save driving time.

Community businesses—especially manufacturers or packagers—may have different kinds of leftover materials that they are willing to donate to the classroom. A fabric store, for example, may have empty cardboard fabric bolts. Construction companies may be willing to donate extra wood scraps or nuts and bolts, and the local plumber may have PVC-piping scraps. Packaging items come in a variety of sizes and shapes. You can find them at appliance stores, grocery stores, or manufacturing sites.

Recycled home-goods stores carry materials such as old windows, doors, doorknobs, furniture, and hardware that have been rescued from demolished houses. Habitat for Humanity is a good affordable source for recycled home goods

▲ Neighborhood thrift stores are some of the best places to find inexpensive household items as well as home décor. Visit these stores frequently, as there are always new items being donated. At times, you may be able to find small pieces of quality, all-wood furniture. Goodwill Industries, the Salvation Army, Habitat for Humanity ReStores, and other thrift stores offer special discount days and coupons for further savings.

▲ Nature is all around us, so child-found natural objects are easy to gather. Armed with paper bags or other containers, take a walk with children and encourage them to fill their containers with leaves, sticks, pinecones, seed pods from trees, rocks, and any other objects they discover.

Thoughtful and Intentional Container Selection

To fully and effectively develop a perspective of thinking about containers as visual objects that spark interest and engagement in children, it is important to realize that our choice of containers may be affected by conventional beliefs of classroom organization that we have developed over time. For example, you may think that all materials should be explicitly sorted and labeled for children or that certain materials should be available in only certain parts of the classroom. These beliefs are neither right nor wrong, but they do affect our container choices and how we make them available to children. For instance, if we believe that sorting and labeling materials is important to classroom organization, we will likely select a conventional compartmentalized block shelf rather than assorted barrels. Or, we may provide color-coded plastic containers filled with identical art tools in the art center, but we may not think to use such containers in other locations for other purposes.

In one preschool art studio, children consistently selected watercolors over any other medium, despite having a variety of art mediums available. The studio's art materials were visible to the children and were neatly arranged and color coded—the red crayons were placed in a red container, the yellow crayons in a yellow container, the blue crayons in a blue container, and so on. Despite the neat arrangement, the teacher was concerned that the children were not using all the materials available, so she decided to rearrange the area.

▲ Beautiful tins hold loose parts in housekeeping.

A pegboard divider, typically used to separate two areas in a classroom, was bolted together with washers, nuts, and bolts to make a triangular stand. She screwed wire cabinet dividers to the stand at different heights and placed small white plastic cups in the holders. The cups held assortments of colored pencils, crayons, chalk, and other writing utensils. She placed the triangular stand holding the cups in the middle of the room to provide reasonable access from all the areas in the classroom.

Once the pegboard container was in place, there was a remarkable difference in the children's choice of art media. Children became more actively engaged with different types of materials. They would walk over to the triangular stand, pick out a cup, move over to an art surface such as a table, floor, or easel, and explore with various writing utensils. The change in children's behavior could be attributed to the fact that this unconventional container was convenient. By bringing them out into the open, the materials became more accessible and easy to use. There was no need for children to dig into a shelf to pull out a red crayon from the back and risk knocking over the other crayons in the front. For the teacher, this experience challenged her beliefs about sorting art supplies by color to increase accessibility.

Containers have at least two jobs: to store learning materials and to attract children to their contents. When you view containers through this lens, a new world opens up. Think about your classroom for a moment and consider all the containers in your space. Most likely, your thoughts immediately focus on the bins and baskets positioned on the classroom's shelves and tabletops. Containers, however, are much more than bins and baskets. Use containers to spark children's interest and engagement with the containers' contents. With this in mind, use the four C's of container selection for guidelines and inspiration when selecting classroom containers.

- Capture children's attention.

- Select convenient containers.

- Connect with activities.

- Use child-created containers.

Select Containers that Capture Children's Attention

To generate children's interest, the container's contents must be visible. Promote visibility by using containers with low, or even no, sides. Because these types of containers do not restrict the view of the contents, they are extremely effective in capturing children's attention. Even though a tree cookie is not a traditional container, for example, it is perfect because it has no sides so whatever it is holding captures children's immediate curiosity and attention.

Another example of a no-sided container is a picture frame. Remove the glass and backing and any wire or hardware from the frame. Place the empty frame on a table along with a basket of interesting objects for children to create their own masterpieces within the no-sided container.

Use empty frames as containers for three-dimensional objects that children have found or collected. Mount the empty frame to the wall using removable picture-hanging strips. Then, inside the frame, hang child-found objects directly on the wall. The following are readily available 3-D objects to place inside empty frames for the various areas in your classroom.

- **Block Center:** small multicolored wooden blocks
- **Library/Quiet Space:** hardcover books or book jackets from children's storybooks
- **Math/Writing Centers:** large wooden numerals/alphabet letters
- **Art Area:** variety of different sizes and types of paintbrushes

Another idea is to encourage children to contribute their own found objects to place in empty picture frames. Going on nature scavenger hunts at the local park, playground, or even at home is an exciting way to connect children with the classroom's no-sided containers. Children can collect all sorts of interesting natural materials such as rocks and pebbles, pods and seeds, and bark or twigs. And, you don't even need authentic frames—you can easily make frames with sticks and twigs.

Select Convenient Containers

For children's engagement to be sustained, containers must be convenient, functional, and easily accessible. Containers are functional when they are easy for children to access, manage, and transport their contents to other places and spaces in the classroom. If your objective is for children to be able to move the containers around the room, try using medium-sized and easy-to-handle containers made of lightweight materials. Select containers with handles, holes, or places where children can get a good grasp. If, however, you want children to take one item from the container to use, choose heavy containers with holes, slots, or spaces to hold individual objects.

Clay bricks make great immoveable containers for small objects. The holes in the bricks make ideal places to store such writing tools and art supplies as scissors, pencils, markers, and hole punches. These types of containers work well when there are a large number of similar objects to be used by many children. For example, a large tin could be weighted down with rocks, sand, dried popcorn kernels, or coffee beans to hold rulers or paint brushes. The sheer weight, size, and shape of the container communicates to children that the container must remain in place.

▲ Plastic cups and jam jars and lids provide a visual feast of color as they display the markers, pencils, crayons, and oil pastels.

Select Containers that Connect with Activities

Another way to sustain children's interest and engagement is to use containers as part of the classroom's activities as well as storage. Fill a strawberry container, small laundry basket, or colander, for example, with pieces of weaving materials, such as fabric, ribbons, pipe cleaners, and twine, and use the basket as a weaving base. Nested boxes with buttons stored in the smallest box trigger the hands-on activity of sorting and classifying in the different sized boxes. Cookie, muffin tins, or baking trays filled with assorted magnetic pieces are another example of how the container becomes a part of the children's activity.

Containers that both hold materials and promote children's interaction with their contents are very practical because they make direct suggestions to children about the various possibilities in which the materials and the container can be used together. There is no need for adult coaching, demonstration, or instruction, so children's autonomy and initiative are stimulated. In a toddler room, for instance, a preservice teacher offered an inclusive container of materials and the container. This inclusive container—in this case, a colander—and the materials (pipe cleaners) suggested to children the activity of weaving the pipe cleaners through the colander holes. The teacher predicted that the activity would last for five or ten minutes because of the limited attention span of this age group. The activity actually continued for twenty minutes of sustained and focused engagement with the container.

Use Child-Created Containers

There are many types of containers children can make. Creating and gifting these containers both promotes children's engagement with a variety of materials and honors their work when it is displayed and used by others.

One way to make a classroom container using buttons is to make a button tray. Simply mix liquid glue with sand, and press the glue into the bottom of a tray. Then press buttons into the glue-coated tray. You can also use plaster of Paris for this project.

Child-created containers can be made with clean microwave dinner trays and bowls. Children can glue fabric, yarn, and twine to make wonderful classroom containers. Something important happens when child-created containers are actively used and enjoyed: Children experience self-satisfaction and a sense of pride when their containers become an important part of the classroom.

The four C's of container selection all have one thing in common: They are unconventional. It is human nature to notice something that is different. Conventional containers create a sterile environment, while unconventional containers awaken a sense of energy and excitement. Think critically about the containers in your classroom. Do they primarily hold objects or do they also grab the children's attention and entice them to explore the contents? Are the containers unusual? Do they evoke curiosity?

Classroom Container Checklist

To begin thinking about your classroom containers, conduct a survey of your classroom by asking the following questions:	YES	NO
Do you have more primary-colored plastic containers than containers made from natural materials?		
Do you have more conventional containers, such as boxes, bins, and baskets, than unconventional containers, such as no-sided, repurposed, and child-made containers?		
Are there more containers similar in type, such as clear plastic totes or coordinated sets of bins and baskets, than containers that have variety, such as an assortment of varying sizes, shapes, colors, and materials?		

If you answered yes to at least two of the questions, it is time to reconsider the purpose of the containers in your classroom.

It's easy to find nontraditional containers once you embrace the idea that the purpose of containers is to attract children's engagement with their contents rather than simply holding objects. Use this new lens when rummaging through garage sales, thrift stores, or even your own basement or attic. Think about how you could reposition or repurpose found objects into useful and captivating containers. The following ideas can help you think about containers from this new perspective.

▲ Wooden cups placed on top of a tree cookie and woven placemat make beautiful containers for writing tools.

▼ Oil and vinegar shakers are great containers for paint and colored water.   ▼ A child's rain boot makes a fun container for smaller toys.

▲ Use a divided box as a container for paint bottles and brushes.

▲ A cupcake display rack easily holds scissors as well as small pieces of paper for practicing cutting skills.

▲ Transform a small log into a container simply by cutting holes large enough to hold crayons or markers.

▲ Use mini-cake pans for containers of loose parts and small objects.

▲ Mason jars are hard to break and have the perfect-sized openings for small paintbrushes and pencils.

Authenticity with Kitchen Gadgets and Home Décor

The quality of the materials placed in an early childhood environment sends a strong signal about our beliefs and how we view young children—as either incompetent or competent. Viewing children as competent individuals means introducing them to authentic materials. By doing this, we are sending the message: You are important enough to share the best we have.

Step into a housekeeping center filled with inexpensive plastic versions instead of authentic objects, and you will find a cool, artificial mood. Step into a housekeeping center stocked with wooden plates, a metal tea pot, cloth napkins, thick coffee mugs, placemats, pot holders, and a colander, and there is a homelike warmth.

Children are capable of working with authentic and sometimes breakable objects, such as a mason jar filled with markers or fine-haired Chinese paintbrushes. All it takes is gentle guidance and the confidence that the child will learn. If something breaks, there is an opportunity to clean up and learn from the mishandling. It is critical that we give children the space, time, and authentic materials to grow into the capable human beings we know them to be.

Providing real kitchenware in the dramatic play area creates interest and engagement with young children. Notice what objects the teacher used to set the table for dinner: a linen tablecloth with a lace doily, wicker plate chargers, wooden bowls, plastic drinking cups, linen napkins, and real silverware. All of these authentic materials have a rich palette of textures and weight. Additionally, the kitchen's back shelf holds metal food tins and cooking utensils ready for play.

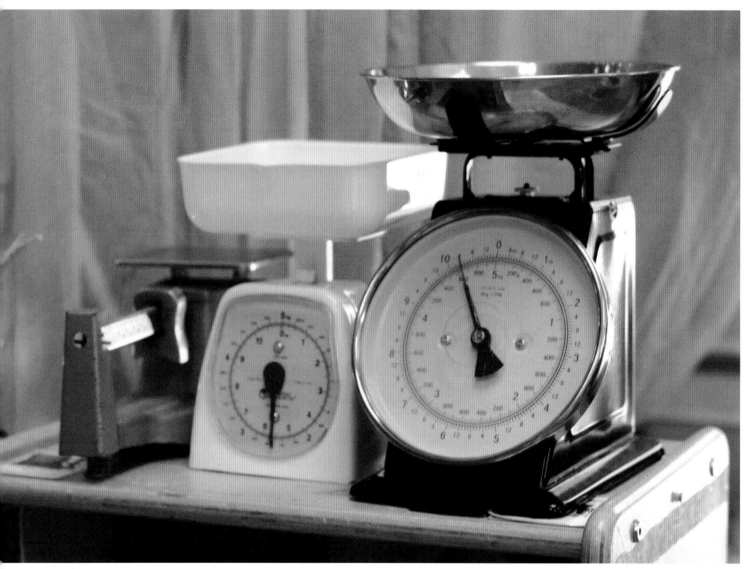

▲ Authentic kitchen scales are a wonderful addition to the science center for weighing and comparing natural items such as rocks and nuts.

There are three categories of kitchenware: cookware, ovenware, and service ware. Cookware is intended for use on top of the stove or for the preparation of food. Ovenware is intended for use inside the oven. Service ware includes those containers we use for serving the food and decorating the table. All three categories of kitchenware make perfect additions to the home living area in the early childhood classroom.

Three Categories of Kitchenware

Cookware

- Sauce pans
- Frying pans
- Whisks
- Measuring cups
- Tongs
- Bamboo steamer
- Mixing bowls
- Strainers
- Kitchen scales
- Spatulas
- Woks
- Wooden spoons
- Funnels
- Potato mashers
- Egg-poacher pans
- Cookie cutters
- Scrapers

Ovenware

- Cake pans
- Bundt-cake pans
- Pie pans
- Bread pans
- Cookie sheets
- Muffin tins
- Casserole dishes

Service Ware

- Glasses and cups
- Plates and bowls
- Vases
- Trays
- Napkin rings
- Placemats
- Silverware
- Tablecloths
- Napkins

Authentic Furniture

Authentic furniture, which is any piece of furniture originally created for a home environment, is typically designed for adult use and not for children. Sprinkling authentic furniture throughout the classroom brings a sense of comfort and warmth, creating a homelike space for children to enjoy.

▲ An open piano bench with an acrylic mirror attached turns into a sensory table. Be sure to attach the piano lid to the wall to avoid pinched fingers.

▲ A coffee table becomes an office desk.

▲ A side table is transformed into a kitchen.

▲ An old end table makes a beautiful addition to the home living area.

▲ An entertainment television stand becomes a writing center.

▲ A wooden cable spool and chair serve as a peace table for resolving conflicts.

▲ A shelf becomes a kitchen center.

▲ An authentic make-up dresser promotes conversations and imaginative play.

▲ By using the drawer for storage, an end table makes a perfect manipulative area.

Variety of Chair Choices

In real life, there are ever so many different types of chairs or options for seating: couches, rocking chairs, recliners, beach chairs, dining room chairs, ottomans, high chairs, stools, swings, lawn chairs, booster seats, beanbag chairs, office chairs, and benches. These chairs are small, large, tall, short, and everything in between. They are made from all sorts of different materials such as leather, textiles, wicker, wood, and plastic. They come in every color of the rainbow and an equal number of patterns and designs.

Think about your home. How many different places are there in your own home or apartment to sit? Are there several different types of chairs? Do you sit on certain chairs to do certain things, such as watch television, eat dinner, or work on the computer? Do you sometimes move your chairs to different areas of the house, such as when you are having a big dinner party or watching a big game on television? In real life, there are many seating options and an equal amount of flexibility. Yet, in the early childhood classroom—which is supposed to be homelike, comfortable, and inviting—the choice of seating is noticeably limited.

Although licensed centers are required to have one chair for each student who is physically able to sit on his own, there are few other requirements for seating. Some classrooms may have the child-size couch and perhaps a small matching side chair for the home living area. Some classrooms might even have a child's rocking chair and perhaps an adult rocking chair. Other than these typical seating options, however, there's not much choice when it comes to chairs in the early childhood classroom. Just like adults, children need opportunities to make choices. Give children plenty of options, especially in selecting a place to sit.

When it comes to selecting chairs for the classroom, our minds automatically go to the early childhood catalog. But there are many other places to find interesting, varied, and fairly inexpensive chairs. Be on the lookout for chairs at garage and yard sales, recycle shops, estate auctions, the local home-goods store, and Grandma's basement.

▲ A full-sized chair encourages dramatic play.

7

Do-It-Yourself Projects for the Classroom

Upcycled and Repurposed Furniture

Repurposing old furniture not only saves money and is environmentally friendly, but it also adds authenticity to a space. In this section of the book, you will find do-it-yourself projects that range from beginner to more advanced. Please consider these projects a starting point; by no means should you feel limited by these ideas or instructions! Use the following ideas to spark your own potential in transforming discarded or damaged furniture into wonderful, authentic additions to the classroom.

Tips for Locating Authentic Materials

- Watch for furniture placed on the curb for giveaway or removal. A broken chair's legs can even be used.
- Check your local thrift store from time to time for damaged donations. Often you can buy these for a few dollars or even get them for free.
- Keep an open mind. A nightstand with a broken door can be transformed into a kitchen table or whatever you can imagine.
- Ask friends and family to look in their garages, attics, or basements. There is a treasure trove of objects you can transform.

DOOR OR WINDOW SHADOW-BOX TABLE

Skill Level: Intermediate

A curiosity table is an enticing and hands-on addition to the classroom. Use an old window and a wooden pallet to create a place for children to gather and draw or investigate and discover new things.

Materials

- Old window with glass removed
- Plexiglas to replace glass removed
- Pallet or plywood (at least ½ inch thick)
- 1" x 6" piece of wood, long enough to equal the total outside dimensions of the window you have chosen to use
- Deck screws
- Wood glue
- 4 table legs and hardware
- 2 6-inch hinges
- 1 6-inch latch
- 80-grit sandpaper
- 1½-inch nails
- Masking tape
- Paint

Tools Needed

- Battery-operated drill
- Hand crosscut saw
- Phillips or regular screwdriver (depending on the types of screws)
- Hammer
- Carpenter's square
- Measuring tape
- Paintbrush

How to Do It

1. Measure the length and width of the window. This will give you the dimensions you will use to build the table.

2. Cut a piece of Plexiglas to the dimensions of the window. (Most stores that sell Plexiglas will cut it for you.)

3.   To create the sides of the window box, cut the 1" x 6" piece of wood into four pieces that are the same lengths as each side of the window. The two longer pieces should be the same length as the long side of the window. The two short pieces should be same length as the short side of the window minus 2 inches to ensure that the small pieces will fit inside the long ends of the box. **Tip:** Use a carpenter's square when you measure to be sure both ends are square before cutting.

4.   Assemble the box with the pieces of 1" x 6" wood on a hard, flat surface, such as an even floor or tabletop. Place the short pieces of wood inside the long pieces. The long ends should overlap the short ends.

5.   Hold the corners of the box together with masking tape.

6.   Open each corner separately, apply wood glue to both sides of the corner, and press the joints firmly back together. Be sure corners are square. Let dry.

7.   Holding the box together with the masking tape, drill 1½-inch-long holes for wood screws on each side of the box where short end meets the long end of the box. The long end should overlap the shorter end.

8.   Using a battery-charged drill, run wood screws into the drill holes you have created until each screw head is flush with the board. At this point, the window size is the same size as the box you have created, and all corners are square.

9.   Wrap 80-grit sandpaper around a piece of wood, and sand all rough edges that may cause splinters.

10. Create the table's bottom by cutting a piece of plywood the same size as the box you have built. The wood used for this bottom should be strong and thick enough to screw legs into. (We used an old pallet to create the bottom.)

11. Connect the table's bottom to the box you have created. Spread a bead of glue around the perimeter of the bottom. Be sure the box and the bottom are square. Place the box on the bottom, and press them firmly together. Let dry.

12. Attach the bottom to the box with 1½-inch nails, putting at least eight to ten nails per side.

13. Using the leg hardware (included with the legs when you buy them), attach the hardware to each corner of the bottom of the table with the screws provided.

14. Attach the legs.

15. Paint the table as desired. Let dry.

16. To prevent the Plexiglas from cracking, drill 1-inch pilot holes every few inches around the perimeter of the Plexiglas.

17. Screw the Plexiglas to the top side of the window frame.

18. Attach the two hinges and one clasp where desired.

19. Fill the box with interesting nature items and found objects.

END-TABLE STOVE

Skill Level: Intermediate

Dramatic play is a favorite activity for young children. Children love to take on adult roles and pretend to be parents or professionals. You can turn a small bedside table into a sweet child's kitchen. Notice the use of real pots and pans and kitchen accessories. These instructions will tell you how to make either a stove or a sink, but you can combine the two if the end table is large enough.

Materials

- End table or nightstand (thrift-store find)
- Semi-gloss paint
- 6 S hooks
- Wood glue
- 2 burner knobs
- 2 burner covers or plywood
- Nails and screws

- 80-grit sandpaper
- Pots and pans
- Kitchen tools, such as spatulas, large spoons, and tongs
- Metal bowl
- Faucet

Tools Needed

- Electric sander
- Jigsaw
- Hammer
- Screwdriver
- Battery-powered drill
- Paintbrush

How to Do It

1. Sand the nightstand with 80-grit sandpaper.

2. Paint the nightstand and let dry.

3. For the stove's burners, cut a circle (or possibly two circles, depending on the size of the nightstand) from plywood. Paint the circles white and let dry. Alternatively, you could use two burner covers.

4. Drill a hole in the center of each burner circle (or cover), and attach the burners to the top of the nightstand with screws.

5. Drill ⅛-inch-diameter holes in the burner knobs, and then screw the burner knobs to the front of the nightstand.

6. For the sink, trace around the metal bowl on the top of the table. Cut a hole that is slightly smaller than the diameter of the bowl. Set the bowl into the hole.

7. Cut holes in the top of nightstand to accommodate the faucet and fit in place. There is a nut that comes with the faucet fittings to use in order to affix the faucet to cabinet.

8. Hang S hooks on the side. Hang the pots and pans and utensils from the S hooks.

BREADBOX WRITING DESK

Skill Level: Beginner

Children's concentration will be enhanced when you add an individual space to your writing center by upcycling an old breadbox and a child-sized table.

Materials

- Old breadbox with roller top
- Small table
- 120-grit sandpaper
- Clear gloss or white paint
- Wood glue
- Phillips or flathead screws
- Paper
- Pencils
- Crayons
- Markers

Tools Needed

- Battery-operated drill
- Phillips or regular screwdriver (depending on screws)

How to Do It

1. Glue and screw the breadbox to the top of the table.

2. Sand everything with 120-grit sandpaper.

3. Paint with a clear gloss or white paint. Let dry.

4. Fill the breadbox with a variety of writing materials, and place the desk in your writing area.

SIDE-TABLE DESK

Skill Level: Beginner

Sometimes children work better when they have a quiet space to think and create. A nightstand and an old tabletop can be combined to create a writing or homework area for the classroom.

Materials

- Small nightstand
- Wood board, old tabletop, or cabinet door that is longer and wider than the top of the nightstand
- 2 table legs
- 2 top plate hardware sets that include screws
- Semi-gloss paint
- Primer
- 120-grit sandpaper
- Optional: child's chair
- Phillips or flathead screws
- Glue

Tools Needed

- Battery-operated drill
- Phillips or flathead screwdriver
- Hand or electric saw
- Paintbrush

How to Do It

1. Cut the wood board or cabinet door to match the width of the nightstand.
2. Remove the drawers and drawer hardware from the nightstand.
3. Cut the table legs to match the height of the desk.
4. Attach the desktop with glue and screws to the nightstand. Let dry.
5. Screw the two top plates underneath the desktop's overhanging edge at the spots where the two legs will be attached.
6. Attach the legs.
7. Sand and prime. Let dry.
8. Paint as desired. Let dry.

PALLET CALENDAR

Skill Level: Beginner

Pallets are versatile and can be used for a variety of projects. Upcycle an old pallet to create an interactive calendar for children to enjoy.

Materials

- Wooden pallet
- 2 eye hooks
- 42 wooden clothespins
- Hot-glue sticks
- Clear adhesive paper
- Paper squares
- Pen or marker

Tools Needed

- Hot-glue gun
- Measuring tape or ruler

How to Do It

1. On the pallet, measure out and mark with a pen a grid with six rows of seven places each.
2. Hot glue a clothespin to each of the spaces in the grid.
3. Have children make days-of-the-week tags.
4. For durability, cover each tag with adhesive paper, and glue each one to the pallet at the top of the appropriate column.
5. Screw the two hooks to the top edge of the pallet, and hang the calendar at the children's eye level.

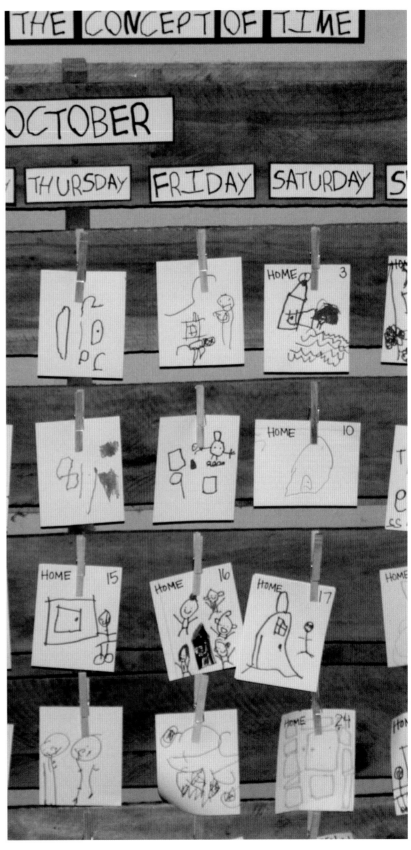

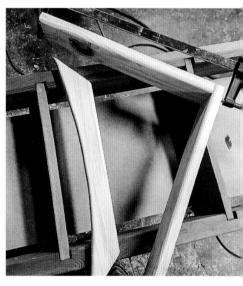

LADDER CANOPY

Skill Level: Intermediate

Something as simple as a ladder can turn a space into a cozy, magical place. You can do this by upcycling an old bunk-bed ladder, but any ladder would work.

Materials

- 1 wooden ladder
- 2 L brackets
- Molly bolts and screws
- Glue
- Paint or wood stain
- Sheer material
- Twinkle lights

Tools Needed

- Screwdriver
- Paintbrush
- Battery-powered drill

How to Do It

1. Drill pilot holes into the ladder approximately 1/3 of the way from each end.
2. Attach L brackets to the ladder at the spots where you've drilled the pilot holes.
3. Stain or paint the ladder, and let it dry, then add a clear coat. Let dry completely.
4. Attach the ladder to a wall with molly bolts and screws.
5. Wrap the fabric around the ladder to create a canopy. For extra sparkle, add twinkle lights.

WOODEN CRATE SHELVING

Skill Level: Beginner

Storage is always a hot commodity in the early childhood classroom. Repurposing wooden crates can create a functional and interesting storage shelf.

Materials

- 6 wooden crates
- Plywood
- White paint
- Wood stain
- Clear coat semi-gloss
- Nails or flathead or Phillips screws
- Wood glue
- 120-grit sandpaper

Tools Needed

- Hammer (if using nails)
- Screwdriver (if using screws)
- Paintbrush
- Sander

How to Do It

1. Decide on the arrangement for the crates. You could stack them, place them side by side, or both.

2. Glue and pin together the crates with nails or screws in the desired arrangement.

3. Prime the crates and let dry.

4. Paint the crates and let dry.

5. Measure the width of the connected crates, and cut the plywood to be slightly longer and wider than the dimensions of the connected crates. This piece will form a top shelf.

6. Set the wood on top of the crates so that it is flush with the back edge of the crates but hangs over the other three edges, and attach the top with glue and screws. Let dry.

7. Sand and stain or paint the top. Let dry.

8. When dry, add clear coat to the top and crates. Let dry.

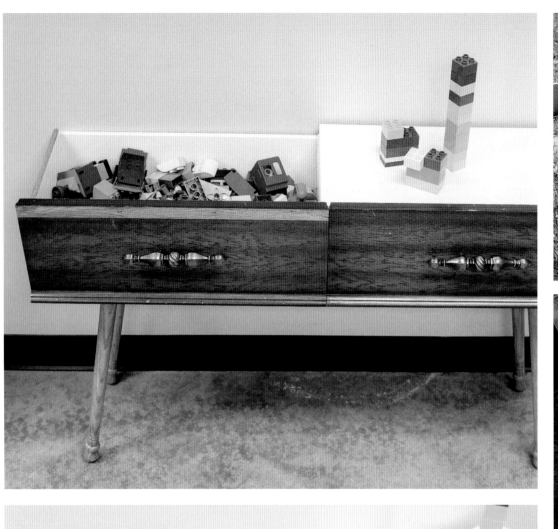

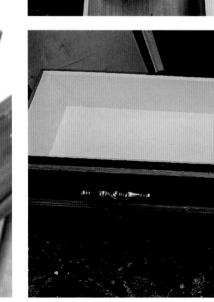

TWO-DRAWER LOOSE PARTS PLAY STATION

Skill Level: Intermediate

This clever idea will help you create more places to store manipulatives and small loose parts; it will also give you more surface area where children can design and build. You can make this multiuse table by upcycling two drawers from an old dresser and four legs from an old table.

Materials

- 2 drawers
- Plywood
- 4 table legs
- 4 angle top plates
- Angle-plate hardware
- White paint
- Clear-coat finish
- Glue
- Loose parts, such as connecting bricks, nuts and bolts, and so on

Tools Needed

- Screwdriver
- Paintbrush
- Battery-powered drill

How to Do It

1. Screw and glue both drawers side by side together as evenly as possible. Let dry.

2. Cut a piece of plywood to the dimensions needed to cover the top of one drawer.

3. Glue the plywood to the top of one of the drawers. Let dry.

4. Screw the angle top plates on the bottoms of the drawers where you want the legs.

5. Screw the legs in.

6. Paint the insides of the drawers. Let dry.

7. Finish with clear coat all over the table. Let dry.

8. Fill the open side of the table with loose parts for the children to explore.

CHAIR KITCHEN

Skill Level: Beginner

If you have an old child-sized chair around that is still stable, you can upcycle it along with some knobs to make this chair kitchen.

Materials

- Wooden chair
- 3 pieces of plywood
- Glue
- 120-grit sandpaper
- Paint or wood stain
- Clear coat semi-gloss
- Stove knobs
- Screws

Tools Needed

- Saw
- Drill
- Paintbrush

How to Do It

1. Cut three pieces of plywood. Two of them should be the width of the back slats of the chair. The third piece should be the width of the front of the chair from the inner edge of one leg to the inner edge of the other leg.

2. Sand all three pieces and add clear coat. Let dry.

3. On the piece for the front of the chair, screw on the stove knobs.

4. From plywood, cut four circles and paint them white. Let dry. These will be the stove burners.

5. Paint the chair white and the seat of the chair with the wood stain. Let dry.

6. Glue the burners to the chair seat. Let dry.

7. Glue the two short wood pieces to the back of the chair. Let dry.

8. Glue the wood piece with the knobs right below the chair seat on the front of the chair. Let dry.

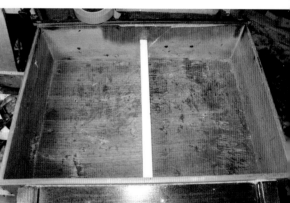

DRAWERS EASEL

Skill Level: Intermediate

If you need more vertical play space in your classroom, you can create this unique easel by upcycling two dresser drawers and some chair legs.

Materials

- Drawer
- 2 chair legs
- 1" x 4" pine board, 4' long
- Screws
- White paint
- Chalkboard paint

Tools Needed

- Screwdriver
- Saw
- Paintbrush

How to Do It

1. Remove the front frame and legs of an old chair (the dark wood legged easel) or remove two legs from an old chair (the white legged easel).

2. Attach the chair legs either by gluing and screwing to the side of the drawer to the legs (white leg example) or attaching the legs under the drawer (dark leg example). Let dry. Note: These easels are not designed to stand on their own. They must be affixed to the wall.

3. Optional: Cut and glue the 1" x 4" pine board to create a center divider in the middle of the drawer. Let dry.

4. Paint one side of the drawer white and the other side with chalkboard paint. Let dry.

5. These easels must be affixed against a wall using screws in all four corners of the drawer..

BOOK BIN

Skill Level: Beginner

If you have an unstable bookshelf, it's not a total loss. You can upcycle a small section of it to create a handy book bin. This build will make a small bin or shelf.

Materials

- Bookshelf
- Plywood
- 1' x 1½' pine board
- 4 chair legs
- 4 top plates to attach the chair legs
- Screws and nails
- White paint
- Clear coat semi-gloss

Tools Needed

- Saw
- Hammer
- Screwdriver
- Measuring tape

How to Do It

1. Place the bookshelf on its back, the cubbies facing up.

2. Measure the dimensions of the space at the bottom of the first cubby. Cut four pieces of pine board to make a square that fits snugly in that space, and glue the boards to the bottom. Let dry.

3. Repeat step 2 for the rest of the cubbies. Let dry.

4. Cut three plywood squares to fit snugly on top of the pine-board squares.

5. Paint the plywood squares white. Let dry.

6. Nail the plywood squares on top of the pine-board squares.

7. Turn the bookshelf over so that the cubbies face down. Attach the four top plates in each corner for the legs, as seen in the photo.

8. Screw the legs on, and add a clear coat to the legs. Let it dry.

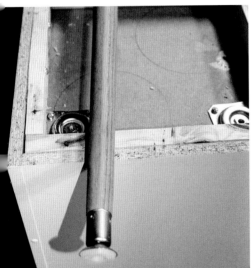

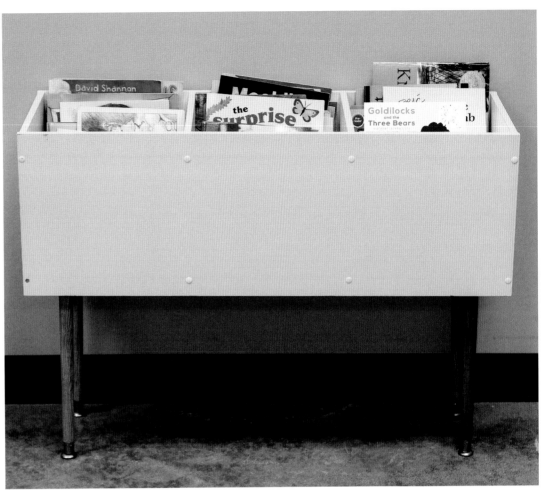

Final Thoughts

At times, we may believe we are ordinary; however, we have the capacity and capability to be much more. For the good of all children, we must strive to be extraordinary—especially in our classrooms. This book is intended to help you transform an ordinary classroom into an extraordinary place for children to be, grow, and learn.

In the world of Reggio Emilia, this idea of extraordinary is thought of as rich normality. *Rich normality*, according to Margie Cooper in her article "Is Beauty a Way of Knowing?" is often used to describe the essence of Reggio environments and includes the physical, social, emotional, and cognitive elements. It is our hope that after reading this book, the notion of rich normality will be in your thoughts and plans for your own classroom design. It is our hope that the suggestions, ideas, and projects included in this book will encourage you to go beyond the ordinary.

Our Inspiration

Our grandchildren give us inspiration and through their eyes we see possibilities to create childhood memories that they will look back on with warmth.

Pictured below:
Jody Martin's grandchildren: Wyatt, Waverly, Shea, Hope, Liberty, Honor, and Roman
Sally Haughey's grandchildren: Kaiden and Kamden
Sandra Duncan's granddaughter: Sierra Elizabeth

References and Inspirations

Aarssen, Cassandra. 2017. *Real Life Organizing: Clean and Clutter-Free in 15 Minutes a Day.* Coral Gables, FL: Mango Publishing Group.

Armstrong, Linda. 2012. *Family Child Care Homes: Creative Spaces for Children to Learn.* St. Paul, MN: Redleaf.

Bachelard, Gaston. 1994. *The Poetics of Space: The Classic Look at How We Experience Intimate Places.* New York, NY: Orion Press.

Bar, Moshe, and Maital Neta. 2006. "Humans Prefer Curved Visual Objects." *Psychological Science* 17(8): 645–648.

Barrett, Peter, and Lucinda Barrett. 2010. "The Potential of Positive Places: Senses, Brain, and Spaces." *Intelligent Buildings International* 2(3): 218–228.

Barrett, Peter, Fay Davies, Yufan Zhaug, and Lucinda Barrett. 2016. "The Holistic Impact of Classroom Space on Learning in Specific Subjects." *Environment and Behavior* 49(4): 425–451.

Boyatzis, Chris, and Reenu Varghese. 1994. "Children's Emotional Association with Color." *The Journal of Genetic Psychology* 3(1): 77–85.

Buchan, Niki. 2016. *A Practical Guide to Nature-Based Practice.* London, UK: Featherstone.

Capizzano, Jeffrey, and Regan Main. 2002. "Many Young Children Spend Long Hours in Child Care." *Snapshots III of America's Families.* https://www.urban.org/sites/default/files/publication/51526/311154-Many-Young- Children-Spend-Long-Hours-in-Child-Care.PDF

Carlson, Frances. 2013. "Retail 101." *Exchange* 35(210): 28–30.

Chard, Sylvia, and Yvonne Kogan. 2009. *From My Side: Being a Child.* Lewisville, NC: KPress.

Conner, Bobbi. 2007. *Unplugged Play: No Batteries. No Plugs. Pure Fun.* New York, NY: Workman Publishing.

Cooper, Margie. 2009. "Is Beauty a Way of Knowing?" *Innovations in Early Childhood Education: The International Reggio Emilia Exchange* 16(3): 1–9.

Curtis, Deb and Margie Carter. 2015. *Designs for Living and Learning: Transforming Early Childhood Environments.* St. Paul, MN: Redleaf Press.

Darragh, Johnna. 2008. "The View from the Door: Entryways as an Essential Aspect of Environmental Design." *Exchange* 30(184): 22–25.

Day, Christopher. 2007. *Environment and Children: Passive Lessons from the Everyday Environment*. Burlington, MA: Architectural Press.

Dazkir, Seda, and Marilyn A. Read. 2012. "Furniture Forms and Their Influence on Our Emotional Responses toward Interior Environments." *Environment and Behavior* 44(5): 722–732.

DEC/NAEYC. 2009. *Early Childhood Inclusion: A Joint Position Statement of the Division for Early Childhood (DEC) and the National Association for the Education of Young Children (NAEYC)*. Chapel Hill, NC: The University of North Carolina, FPG Child Development Institute.

Deviney, Jessica, et al. 2010. *Inspiring Spaces for Young Children*. Silver Spring, MD: Gryphon House.

Deviney, Jessica, et al. 2010. *Rating Observation Scale for Inspiring Environments: A Companion Observation Guide for Inspiring Spaces for Young Children*. Silver Spring, MD: Gryphon House.

Doorley, Scott, and Scott Witthoft. 2012. *Make Space: How to Set the Stage for Creative Collaboration*. Hoboken, NJ: John Wiley and Sons.

Dotseth-Hall, Alycia. 2015. "Making Time for Tummy Time." *Exchange* 37(225): 64–67.

Dudek, Mark. 2005. *Children's Spaces*. Burlington, MA: Architectural Press.

Duncan, Sandra. 2011. "Breaking the Code: Changing Our Thinking about Children's Environments." *Exchange* 33(200): 13–17.

Duncan, Sandra. 2013. "It's Already There: Children's Passion for Learning." *Exchange* 35(214): 51.

Duncan, Sandra. 2014. "Clatter in the Classroom." Community Playthings. http://www.communityplaythings.com/resources/articles/2014/clatter-in-the-classroom

Duncan, Sandra, and Deb Lawrence. 2010. "The Power of Classroom Dispositions." *Exchange* 32(196): 51–54.

Duncan, Sandra, and Mickey MacGillivray. 2014. "Metal: A Perfect Play Material for Children's Improvisation." *Exchange* 36(220): 57–60.

Duncan, Sandra, and Jody Martin. 2018. *Bringing the Outside In: Ideas for Creating Nature-Based Classroom Experiences for Young Children*. Lincoln, NE: Exchange Press.

Duncan, Sandra, Jody Martin, and Rebecca Kreth. 2016. *Rethinking the Classroom Landscape: Creating Environments that Connect Young Children, Families, and Communities*. Lewisville, NC: Gryphon House.

Duncan, Sandra, and Michelle Salcedo. 2012. "Are Your Children in Times Square? Moving from Sensory Overload to Sensory Engagement." *Exchange* 208(6): 48–52.

Edwards, Carolyn, Lella Gandini, and George Forman, eds. 2012. *The Hundred Languages of Children: The Reggio Emilia Experience in Transformation.* Santa Barbara, CA: Praeger.

Engelbrecht, Kathie. 2003. *The Impact of Color on Learning.* Chicago, IL: Perkins and Will. https://pdfs.semanticscholar. org/370a/5af3c86c1255defe3a1e83a13e9950958800.pdf?_ga=2.228612124.1619670969.1523280921- 686236546.1523280921

Epstein, Ann. 2007. *The Intentional Teacher: Choosing the Best Strategies for Young Children's Learning.* Washington, DC: NAEYC.

Fishbaugh, Angela Schmidt. 2011. *Celebrate Nature! Activities for Every Season.* St. Paul, MN: Redleaf.

Fisher, Anna V., Karrie E. Godwin, and Howard Seltman. 2014. "Visual Environment, Attention, Allocation, and Learning in Young Children: When Too Much of a Good Thing May Be Bad." *Psychological Science* 25(7): 1362–1370.

Gaines, Kristi, and Zane Curry. 2011. "The Inclusive Classroom: The Effects of Color on Learning and Behavior." *Journal of Family and Consumer Sciences Education* 29(1): 46–57.

Galinsky, Ellen. 2010. *Mind in the Making: The Seven Essential Life Skills Every Child Needs.* New York, NY: HarperCollins.

Gibson, James. 1986. *The Ecological Approach to Visual Perception.* New York, NY: Psychology Press.

Goldhagen, Sarah. 2017. *Welcome to Your World: How the Built Environment Shapes Our Lives.* New York, NY: HarperCollins.

Greenman, Jim. 2004. "The Experience of Space: The Pleasure of Space." *Exchange* 26: 36–37.

Greenman, Jim. 2017. *Caring Spaces, Learning Places: Children's Environments That Work!* Lincoln, NE: Exchange Press.

Gussow, Alan. 1972. *A Sense of Place: The Artist and the American Land.* San Francisco, CA: Friends of the Earth.

Hall, Ellen Lynn, and Jennifer Kofkin Rudkin. 2011. *Seen and Heard: Children's Rights in Early Childhood Education.* New York, NY: Teachers College Press.

Hammersley, Toni. 2016. *The Complete Book of Home Organization.* San Francisco, CA: Weldon Owen.

Hanscom, Angela. 2016. *Balanced and Barefoot: How Unrestricted Outdoor Play Makes for Strong, Confident, and Capable Children.* Oakland, CA: New Harbinger.

Healy, Maureen. 2008. "The Color of Emotion: Is Color the First Class in Children's Emotional Health?" *Psychology Today.* https://www.psychologytoday.com/blog/creative-development/200812/the-color-emotion

Heiss, Elizabeth Renee. 2004. *Feng Shui for the Classroom: 101 Easy-to-Use Ideas.* Chicago, IL: Zephyr Press.

Hiking Research. 2012. "Time in Nature Is the Real 'Smart Drug' Children Need." Blog. Hiking Research. https://hikingresearch.wordpress.com/tag/nature-and-adhd/

Hiss, Tony. 1990. *The Experience of Place: A New Way of Looking and Dealing with Our Radically Changing Cities and Countryside.* New York, NY: Knopf.

Inan, Hatice Zeynep. 2009. "The Third Dimension in Preschools: Preschool Environments and Classroom Design." *European Journal of Educational Studies* 1(1): 55–66.

Kalia, Soma. 2013. "Colour and Its Effects in Interior Environment: A Review." *International Journal of Advanced Research in Science and Technology* 2(2): 106–109.

Keeler, Rusty. 2008. *Natural Playscapes: Creating Outdoor Play Environments for the Soul.* Redmond, WA: Exchange Press.

Kimmerer, Robin Wall. 2013. *Braiding Sweetgrass: Indigenous Wisdom, Scientific Knowledge, and the Teachings of Plants.* Minneapolis, MN: Milkweed Editions.

Kritchevsky, Sybil, Elizabeth Prescott, and Lee Walling. 1969. *Planning Environments for Young Children.* Washington, DC: NAEYC.

Kubie, Lawrence S. 1961. *Neurotic Distortion of the Creative Process.* New York, NY: Noonday Press/Farrar, Straus, and Giroux.

Kuh, Lisa. 2014. *Thinking Critically about Environments for Young Children: Bridging Theory and Practice.* New York, NY: Teachers College Press.

Kuller, Rikard, et al. 2006. "The Impact of Light and Colour on Psychological Mood: A Cross-Cultural Study of Indoor Work Environments. "*Ergonomics.*" 49(14): 1496–1507.

Leslie, Clare Walker. 2015. T*he Curious Nature Guide: Explore the Natural Wonders All Around You. North Adams*, MA: Storey.

Life.ca. 2016. "Plants Significantly Lower Workplace Stress and Enhances Productivity." Life.ca http://life.ca/2016/04/15/workplace-plants-smarter-healthier/

Lin, Blossom Yen-Ju, Yung-Kai Lin, Cheng-Chieh Lin, and Tien-Tse Lin. 2013. "Job Autonomy, Its Predispositions, and Its Relation to Work Outcomes in Community Health Centers in Taiwan." *Health Promotion International* 28(2): 167–177.

Logrippo, Ro. 1995. *In My World: Designing Living and Learning Environments for the Young*. New York, NY: John Wiley and Sons.

Lohr, Virginia. 2010. "What Are the Benefits of Plants Indoors and Why Do We Respond Positively to Them?" *Acta Horticulturae* 881(2): 675–682.

Louv, Richard. 2006. *Last Child in the Woods: Saving Our Children from Nature-Deficit Disorder*. Chapel Hill, NC: Algonquin.

Lowenstein, George. 1994. "The Psychology of Curiosity: A Review and Reinterpretation." *Psychological Bulletin* 116(1): 75–98.

Martinez, Sylvia Libow, and Gary Stager. 2019. *Invent to Learn: Making, Tinkering, and Engineering in the Classroom*. 2nd ed. Torrance, CA: Constructing Modern Knowledge Press.

Maslow, Abraham. 1954. *Toward a Psychology of Being*. New York, NY: Van Nostrand.

McCurdy, Leyla, Kate Winterbottom, Suril Mehta, and James Roberts. 2010. "Using Nature and Outdoor Activity to Improve Children's Health." *Pediatric and Adolescent Health Care* 40(5): 102–117.

McKim, Robert. 1980. *Experiences in Visual Thinking*. 2nd edition. Pacific Grove, CA: Brooks/Cole.

Miller, Dana L. 2007. "The Seeds of Learning: Young Children Develop Important Skills through Their Gardening Activities at a Midwestern Early Education Program." *Applied Environmental Education and Communication* 6(1): 49–66.

Moore, Robin, and Allen Cooper. 2014. *Nature Play and Learning Places: Creating and Managing Places Where Children Engage with Nature*. Raleigh, NC: Natural Learning Initiative and Reston, VA: National Wildlife Federation.

Murkoff, Heidi. 2014. *What to Expect: The First Year*. 3rd edition. New York, NY: Workman.

NAEYC. 2017. *NAEYC Early Learning Standards and Accreditation Criteria and Guidance for Assessment*. https://www.naeyc.org/sites/default/files/globally-shared/downloads/PDFs/accreditation/early-learning/Standards%20and%20Accreditation%20Criteria%20%26%20Guidance%20for%20Assessment_April%202017_3.pdf

Nafe, Ellen. 2016. *Impacting Early Childhood Student Challenging Behavior through Improving Learning Environment Aesthetics*. Ft. Myers, FL: Nova Southeastern University.

Nicholson, Simon. 1974. "How Not to Cheat Children: The Theory of Loose Parts." *Landscape Architecture* 62(1): 30–34.

Nielson, Karla, and David Taylor. 2007. *Interiors: An Introduction*. 4th edition. New York, NY: McGraw-Hill Education.

Norman, Don. 2013. *The Design of Everyday Things*. New York, NY: Basic Books.

O'Donohue, John. 2004. *Beauty: The Invisible Embrace.* New York, NY: HarperCollins.

Olds, Anita Rui. 2001. *Child Care Design Guide.* New York, NY: McGraw-Hill.

Persing, John, et al. 2003. "Prevention and Management of Positional Skull Deformities in Infants." *Pediatrics* 112(1): 1236–1241.

Petersik, Sherry, and John Petersik. 2012. *Young House Love: 243 Ways to Paint, Craft, Update, and Show Your Home Some Love.* New York, NY: Artisan.

Petrash, Jack. 2002. *Understanding Waldorf Education: Teaching from the Inside Out.* Beltsville, MD: Gryphon House.

Piaget, Jean. 1936. *The Origins of Intelligence in the Child.* London, UK: Routledge and Kegan Paul.

Nair, Prakash, Randall Fielding, and Jeffrey Lackney. 2014. *The Language of School Design: Design Patterns for 21st Century Schools.* 3rd edition. Cambridge, MA: Harvard Education Publishing Group.

Read, Marilyn, Alan Sugawara, and Jeanette A. Brandt. 1999. "Impact of Space and Color in the Physical Environment on Preschool Children's Cooperative Behavior." *Environment and Behavior* 31(3): 413–428.

Real Simple. 2010. *Real Simple: 869 New Uses for Old Things: An Encyclopedia of Innovative Ideas for Everyday Items.* New York, NY: Real Simple Books.

Reggio Children. 2004. *Children, Art, Artists: The Expressive Languages of Children, the Artistic Language of Alberto Burri.* Reggio Emilia, IT: Reggio Children.

Reggio Children International Network. 2014. "Manifesto: Reggio Children International Network, February 2014 (Work in Progress)." *Innovations in Early Education: The International Reggio Emilia Exchange* 21(1): 24–25.

Reid, Kate. 2016. "Counting on It: Early Numeracy Development and the Preschool Child." Australian Council for Educational Research. https://research.acer.edu.au/cgi/viewcontent.cgi?article=1020_context=learning_processes

Rivkin, Mary. 2014. *The Great Outdoors: Advocating for Natural Spaces for Young Children.* Washington, DC: NAEYC.

Rosenow, Nancy. 2012. *Heart-Centered Teaching Inspired by Nature.* Lincoln, NE: Dimensions Educational Research Foundation.

Rushton, Stephen, and Elizabeth Larkin. 2001. "Shaping the Learning Environment: Connecting Developmentally Appropriate Practices to Brain Research." *Early Childhood Education Journal* 29(1): 25–33.

Salcedo, Michelle. 2018. *Uncovering the Roots of Challenging Behavior: Create Responsive Environments Where Young Children Thrive*. Minneapolis, MN: Free Spirit.

Schauss, Alexander. 1979. "Tranquilizing Effect of Color Reduces Aggressive Behavior and Potential Violence." *Journal of Orthomolecular Psychiatry* 8(4): 218–221.

Schiller, Pam. 2015. "Helping Infant and Toddler Caregivers Optimize Development by Being More Intentional in Their Choices of Activities, Interactions, and Experiences." Poster session. NAEYC Professional Development Institute, New Orleans, LA.

Silvia, Paul. 2006. *Exploring the Psychology of Interest*. New York, NY: Oxford University Press.

Silvia, Paul, and Christopher M. Barona. 2009. "Do People Prefer Curved Objects? Angularity, Expertise, and Aesthetic Preference." *Empirical Studies of the Arts* 27(1): 25–42.

Smith, Takiema Bunche, and Louise Ammentorp. 2013. "From Cinder Blocks to Building Blocks: Creating Beautiful Places in Children's Spaces." *Young Children* 68(4): 8–15.

Sorenson, Dina. 2016. "Strong Evidence Found on the Impact of School Design on Learning." American Institute of Architects. Blog. https://network.aia.org/blogs/dina-sorensen/2016/02/18/strong-evidence-found-of-the-impact-of-school-design-on-learning

Soukup, Ruth. 2016. *Unstuffed: Decluttering Your Home, Mind, and Soul*. Grand Rapids, MI: Zondervan.

Sutton, Mary Jo. 2011. "In the Hands and Mind: The Intersection of Loose Parts and Imagination in Evocative Settings for Young Children." *Children, Youth, and Environment* 21(2): 4089–424.

Tarr, Patricia. 2004. "Consider the Walls." *Young Children* 59(3): 88–92.

Taylor, Andrea Fabor, and Francis Kuo. 2009. "Children with Attention Deficits Concentrate Better after Walk in Park." *Journal of Attention Disorders* 12(5): 402–409.

Topal, Cathy, and Lella Gandini. 1999. *Beautiful Stuff! Learning with Found Materials*. Worcester, MA: Davis.

Tuan, Yi-Fu. 1977. *Space and Place: The Perspective of Experience*. Minneapolis, MN: University of Minnesota Press.

Ulrich, Roger S. 1979. "Visual Landscapes and Psychological Well-Being." *Landscape Research* 4(1): 17–23.

Ulrich, Roger S. 1981. "Natural versus Urban Scenes." *Environment and Behavior* 13(5): 523–556.

Ulrich, Roger S. 1984. "View through a Window May Influence Recovery from Surgery." *Science* 224(4647): 420–421. https://mdc.mo.gov/sites/default/files/resources/2012/10/ulrich.pdf

Underhill, Paco. 1999. *Why We Buy: The Science of Shopping.* New York: Simon and Schuster.

U. S. Department of Health and Human Services, Health Resources and Services Administration, Maternal and Child Health Bureau. 2014. *Child Health USA 2014.* Rockville, MD: U. S. Department of Health and Human Services.

Vasandani, Sony. 2015. "Creating Environments that Reduce Children's Stress." *Exchange* 228(6): 40–43.

Verghese, Preeti. 2001. "Visual Search and Attention: A Signal Detection Approach." *Neuron* 31(4): 523–535.

Walker, Morton. 1991. *The Power of Color: The Art and Science of Making Colors Work for You.* New York, NY: Avery.

Whitney, Sue, and Ki Nassauer. 2005. *Decorating Junk Market Style: Repurposed Junk to Suit Any Décor.* Des Moines, IA: Meredith.

Wilson, Ruth A. 2010. "Aesthetics and a Sense of Wonder." *Exchange* 32(3): 24–26.

Wilson, Ruth A. 2014. "Beauty in the Lives of Young Children." *Exchange* 36(2): 36–41.

Wolfarth, Harry, and Catherine Sam. 1982. "The Effects of Color Psychodynamic Environment Modification upon Psycho-Physiological and Behavioral Reactions of Several Handicapped Children." *International Journal of Biosocial Research* 3(1): 30–38.

Wolverton, B. C. 1997. *How to Grow Fresh Air: 50 Houseplants that Purify Your Home or Office.* New York, NY: Penguin

Zane, Linda. 2015. *Pedagogy and Space: Design Inspirations for Early Childhood Classrooms.* St. Paul, MN: Redleaf.

Index